Praise for *The Leap of Your Life*

"A must read for anyone who knows there's a larger life out there for them and is ready to create it!"

—Mark A. Lack, TV Host and Speaker

"There's a lot of noise out there telling you what to do, and how to do it. Unfortunately, few people out there are living it. Tommy Baker is, and *The Leap of Your Life* will give you permission to take ownership of your life and never look back."

—Ryan Michler, Founder of Order of Man

"If you're ready to make that change, that shift, that decision that you know will change your life, but you don't know where to start, Tommy Baker is your answer. Tommy will guide and direct you through *The Leap of Your Life*. Stop waiting for your success, grab this opportunity to be guided by one of the best in the business. Leap!"

—Jay Nixon, Founder, Thrive Fitness

THE LEAP OF YOUR LIFE

TOMMY BAKER

THE LEAP OF YOUR LIFE

HOW TO REDEFINE RISK, QUIT WAITING FOR "SOMEDAY," AND **LIVE BOLDLY**

WILEY

Library of Congress Cataloging-in-Publication Data has been applied for and is on file with the Library of Congress.

ISBN 9781119552536 (Hardcover)
ISBN 9781119552529 (ePDF)
ISBN 9781119552437 (ePub)

Printed in the United States of America
V10008291_021519

For both of my incredible grandmothers, Marjorie and Pepita. For giving me the gift of knowledge, and the belief of possibility.

Contents

Introduction

What are you *waiting* for?

There's a leap in your life you've been putting off, and it's *killing* you. Maybe not literally, but it's killing your spirit. It's killing your belief, your enthusiasm, and the thrill of this one experience we call life. It's killing your energy, vitality, and hope for the future. When those are gone, you might as well be the walking dead.

It's draining your life force, and every day you put it off, you're reminded of how it *hasn't* happened for you yet. And now you're questioning if it *ever* will.

The consequences of not taking your leap are real, and they stare back at you every morning in the mirror. They're reflected in bank statements. They're felt in your body language during time with the people you love. They're wrapped in not on long exhales as you aim to keep it all together.

But worst of all, they're reflected in this tireless voice in the back of your head that won't shut up, asking:

"Is this it? Is this all that's meant for me?"

Now, does this mean I'm certain your life isn't working? No, not at all. Our lives can be working, and we can still have a leap we know we must take. Sometimes, this can be the most precarious circumstance of all: we have everything we've been told we should want, yet something is *still* missing.

And I'm here to tell you what's missing is your leap. But before we get into it all, let's define what a leap is.

The Ingredients of the Leap

You may be wondering: What exactly constitutes a leap? You may be thinking it's abandoning Western life and moving to an ashram in the Himalayas, quitting your accounting gig, launching the new app or parachuting out of a perfectly good airplane at 15,000 feet.

Although all of those sound like fun to me and could be leaps, they don't have to be yours. Sometimes, the leap we have to take seems inconsequential to others and yet leads to a bold moment of no return: reaching out to a recruiter with the hopes of transitioning out of our job, having the tough conversation with our partner, launching the side hustle or finally clicking record and spreading a message with the world.

What matters, then is not necessarily the magnitude of the leap. It's simply that it matters to you, and includes the following:

- **You feel a pull.** You can't explain it, but you feel pulled toward your leap. Much like a magnetic charge, you can try to avoid it, but it comes back stronger than ever.
- **There's a decision.** Your leap involves a decision you've been putting off and will require you to make a bold choice.
- **The stakes are high.** Your leap *matters.* There are real consequences to not making it. There are also endless possibilities by stepping into it.
- **There's an element of risk.** Your leap has a degree of risk, and for now you've chosen to play it "safe" at the expense of your own fulfillment.
- **Not doing it will hurt more than doing it.** Lastly, even though you haven't taken your leap yet, not doing so hurts more than any consequence or perceived failure of taking it.

So, again—what are you waiting for?

If you're here, I already know you're waiting for *something*. Every day you put it off, a part of you withers away, knowing your dreams are on hold as you attempt to live someone else's life. (I use the word *attempt* deliberately, because no matter how hard we try, it'll never quite pan out.)

Playing It Safe Means a Lifetime of Regret

As we begin this adventure, I want you to treat it as such. I'm going to take a wild guess you've read books with similar themes, but you haven't read *this* one. Finishing this book will drive you toward a decision, which won't be shared only between you and me.

There are a few reasons why you may be here right now, and I'm going to tell you why you should stick around:

- **First, you feel a calling for something bolder and bigger for your life**, and you believe it may be possible, but you're finding yourself stuck.
- **Second, you know if you continue on the same path you're on today,** you're going to look back and feel the sinking feeling of regret.
- **Third, you're tired of playing everyone else's game**. For too long, you've done what others told you to do and ignored a part of you that *knew* without question what was right.
- **Last, there's a voice whispering to you during the silent pockets of life** slowly begging you to put yourself on the line and *do it now.*

This voice comes to you when the intensity of life has slowed down. When it can no longer be drowned out in noise, bills, and an unrelenting breaking news cycle, it comes to you. Sometimes it whispers on those long car rides when you're running on autopilot and have the ability to think, during those early mornings right before the chaos of the inbox hits. Or when you're in those in-between moments on the airplane and the perspective of being at 37,000 feet invites some deeper questions.

As long as you fit one, two, or all of those descriptions—you've come to the right place.

By the end of our time together, one of two things will happen:

You'll think everything I said sounded nice, but you won't make the commitment I'm daring you to make—so this might as well be a video game. Except there's no fantasy land, and I'm not nearly as entertaining.

Or, you'll have the spark, the insight, the push required to create something so powerful that the current version of yourself can't imagine it. You'll be brought to your knees (except this time, in an is-this-really-happening way.)

You'll finally take the *Leap of Your Life* and you'll never be the same.

But I've Already Taken a Leap … Is This for Me?

You may be saying to yourself: but I've *already* taken the leap. You launched your business, you moved cross-country, you took the big chance. This can't be for you, right?

Wrong. The fastest way to slide back to mediocrity is to believe life and business are about *one* leap. The truth is, life and business are a series of leaps and micro-leaps as you continue to expand on your journey. Most people assume if they already did a leap, they'll be better prepared for the next one, right?

What I've found is the opposite. In spite of making bold choices in the past, they can feel just as stuck and in fear about their next leap. Often, those with something to lose are less likely to take a leap: taking a chance is easy when you don't have much to lose, but what about when things are working (to a certain degree)?

In working with countless thought leaders, industry trailblazers, and entrepreneurs who have made bold decisions in the past, I've noticed they need a constant reminder to push toward their *next* leap. Otherwise, they slide back to mediocrity, the passion and challenge they once had fizzles, and what once felt like a riveting life has now vanished and become mechanical.

The Greatest Risk (Is Not Taking One)

Starting your own business is risky.

Moving cross-country with no plan is risky.

Asking him or her out before you're ready is risky.

Taking a bold chance on your dreams is risky.

Right?

But what if we're wrong? **What if the *real* risk is putting our dreams on hold, placing them in a box labeled "someday"?**

We've been told to play it safe, to stay in line, and to not dream *too* big, or else we may fail. Follow the secure path and you'll be handsomely rewarded. Since those around you have also bought into this narrative, they'll support you. You'll fit in, and your life's path will be etched in certainty.

And yet, so often we find ourselves on someone else's path, living someone else's dream and trying to live up to the expectations (and approval) of others. **We trade in our calling for our ceiling, our purpose for a paycheck, and our enthusiasm for exhaustion.**

You wake up one day, only to realize you're in the wrong movie wondering how the hell you got there.

Our inability to tolerate even the smallest of risks has led us to live an unfulfilled life. The illusion of security has drained our life force. The calling you felt deep within you started as a wildfire and is now nothing but ashes. What was once a six-lane open highway of possibility has now become a cemetery where dreams go to die.

Reading this book will challenge you to have an open mind, no matter if you consider yourself a brazen risk taker with an entrepreneurial mindset, or your definition of risk is passing someone on the right-hand side of your local freeway at a brisk 66 MPH.

The problem with our perception of risk is simple: we don't take chances during the low-stakes moments of life, so we'll never take them during the high-stakes moments—which means that every single day we're wiring ourselves not to listen to what we know we have to do, so we are unwilling to face the task(s) at hand.

And through that process, we miss facing ourselves.

"Someday" Is Holding You Back

I wrote this book because I have been where you are. I have been stuck and riddled by fear. I have walked the path others wanted for me. I have turned a blind eye to what I knew I had to do, and followed what people told me I should.

It nearly broke me.

Until I *woke up* one New Year's Eve 13-degree night in New York City with tears streaming down my face, painting a vision for a life. For the first time, it felt real. With no plan, no blueprint, and no seven-step system, I took the leap.

Fast-forward to today, and my former life is completely and utterly unrecognizable. I am living every part of my vision, and then some. My obsession is now helping others identify their *leap* and make a bold decision. I've spent over 3,500 + hours in the trenches coaching and consulting others.

I've interviewed over 250 of the world's most accomplished and fulfilled entrepreneurs, leaders, athletes, spiritual teachers, and creatives, and here's the common thread I found among all of them:

They had the courage to listen to the voice inside and take a bold step into the unknown.

Without any guarantees, they bet on themselves. They put their chips in the middle of the poker table known as life, going all in.

And *everything* changed.

In crossing the threshold, they found themselves on the other side with conviction, courage, and a confidence that only comes through stepping into who we really are. We all want to give this experience meaning. We all want to live a purposeful life, engulfed with fulfillment.

The way we get there is simple, yet never easy. **We listen to the calling inside, knowing exactly what we need to do.** We take the jagged, rough, edgy path instead of the perfectly trimmed one. We take the leap calling us, and we never look back. We know there is no guarantee on the other side, except the greatest one of all: **knowing that we played full tilt, all out, and gave it a chance.** We bet on ourselves. We not only had a belief there was something greater out there, but we also had the audacity to step into it.

We lived, dammit!

That's why you're here, and why I'm here. This book will challenge you, and if I do my job, it will force you to answer the tough questions you've been avoiding. It won't be comfortable, because nothing in life that changes us is. I believe you and I have the right to turn this cosmic, blink-of-an eye experience into a canvas for the world to see. A story for generations to read. I want your life to be the greatest story ever told.

This book is broken down into four parts. Part I is where we examine the infinite cost of not taking your leap, and what's *really* holding you back. Armed with a new perspective, you can prepare for your journey in Part II and learn about the essential toolbox you'll need. Part III is about the leap and the different kinds of leaps available to you. Last, Part IV is about ensuring your leap isn't something you do once but instead becomes who you are, while sharing your gifts. You'll create a declaration you'll be sharing to set you off to sail. Throughout, you'll find essential leap tips in each chapter, as well as *#NotesFromTheLeap:* stories from everyday people just like you who radically transformed their lives.

You're here, and you don't know exactly where you're going. *Good.* The unknown is waiting for you, and we've got no time to lose.

If you do it right, you will never be the same.

I

Leaning on the Edge

There are moments in our lives when we summon the courage to make choices that go against reason, against common sense and the wise counsel of people we trust. But we lean forward nonetheless because, despite all risks and rational argument, we believe that the path we are choosing is the right and best thing to do. We refuse to be bystanders, even if we do not know exactly where our actions will lead. This is the kind of passionate conviction that sparks romances, wins battles, and drives people to pursue dreams others wouldn't dare. Belief in ourselves and in what is right catapults us over hurdles, and our lives unfold.

—Howard Schultz

Chapter 1

Daring to Dream

Rate: 833.9 miles per hour. When you're freefalling at this speed, you're only thinking about one thing—the desire to live.

The lead-up to this moment had been a lifetime of bold decisions and redefining risk at every turn. However, none of that mattered now. The radio was silent as the spin became more violent. This silence was deafening.

At 128,000 feet, *everything* is precarious. During an uncontrolled spin, there are only a few possible outcomes. One, blood rushes to the limbs and rids the brain of oxygen. A total blackout results. Unconsciously spinning in space. The alternative is too much blood rushing to the head—and then the pressure inside the skull builds like the pressure in a beer can that's been left in the freezer for too long. Eventually your blood has only one way out—your eyeballs.

No good. When you're spinning uncontrollably for 67 seconds, it feels like an eternity. Alone, every second is your life flashing right before your eyes.

Felix Baumgartner is still here to tell his story—and he regained control in time to accomplish one of the biggest feats in the history of human free fall.

Was it risky? It depends on who you ask.

The Dream of a Lifetime

Just 67 seconds earlier, Felix had been standing on the edge of a custom-made space capsule. Decked out in a handmade spacesuit adorned with the Red Bull logo, the whole world was watching—including his girlfriend, a mother who couldn't bear to watch, and a close circle of friends, all waiting for him 24 miles down. He was about to embark on a lifelong dream—flying. Literally. Ever since he was a little boy, Felix had dreamed of flying. That dream had led to his being known as one of the most accomplished daredevils and stuntmen in history. But *this* was different.

The training had been the most grueling challenge of Felix's life. Several mishaps, technical issues, a nearly fatal training mistake, and a total anxiety shutdown were part of the story. But something was pushing Felix to take this leap. Something within him was guiding him through the dark moments and the sleepless nights.

It would have been easy to rest on his laurels and the YouTube highlights of doing the impossible. He was already a living legend, with nothing to prove. Yet something was pulling at him, and he couldn't afford *not* to listen.

That day at 12:06 p.m. Felix took the *leap of his life* with the entire world watching.

You Have a Quest to Take, Too

I know what you're thinking: you have no plans to jump out of a space capsule and break the speed of sound anytime soon. You're not a daredevil, BASE jumper, or extreme sport athlete. I'm not either, and I'll stick to my two, run-of-the-mill skydiving experiences for now. They were fun, even if the pilot did look like a knockoff version of the guitarist from Metallica and made way too many "this is my first day" jokes.

However, you have a lot more in common with Felix than you think: there's a quest you've been waiting to take. *And every day that passes without you taking it is another chance you'll wind up thinking about what could have been.*

I don't want that for you, but most importantly—*you* don't want that for you. You're here to take the quest, the ride of a lifetime. And your leap is the catalyst to light that quest on fire and write the life story you can't wait to experience. The life you look forward to coming back to after a vacation, *because the thrill of living it exceeds the fantasy of escaping.*

This is exactly where I found myself on a frosty New Year's Eve night when everything changed.

December 31, 2014—10:36 p.m. New York, New York

I'm sitting at a big table in a Manhattan restaurant, surrounded by friends and the sounds of clinking glasses and belly laughter. It's New Year's Eve and the energy is palpable, with busboys gunning in and out at exactly the right time so as not to knock into the waitress who's taking one too many orders.

I'm seated at the table, but I'm not *there*. Something is missing. I've felt this way for a little while now, and I don't know what to do. It's easy to admit you're lost when things *aren't* working. But what about when people think they are? I've had trouble waking up over the past 14 days. For the first time since high school, all I want to do is stay in bed when morning comes around.

The drinks start coming, and I'm on the hook for a ribeye. Bone-in, flown in from Nebraska—or so they say—for a cool $57. I excuse myself, although I'm not sure that any words come out of my mouth.

I find myself walking. It's 13 degrees out, and I'm supposed to be in the bathroom and rejoining the dinner table soon. Except that I'm headed in the opposite direction. I feel the burn of the cold on my face and the windchill in my bones. I don't know where I'm going, yet I know *exactly* where I'm going. I need space. I need to find myself.

Desperately.

I walk until I find an open patch of land—something that looks like an old football field—and instantly I'm drawn to it. Maybe I simply want to relive the glory days that *didn't* happen, but I walk into the field. And without thinking, I'm now sprinting for my life with everything I've got—Michael Kors pants and shirt included. I repeat the cycle of walking and sprinting a few times, not thinking about who may be witnessing this: it is *New York*, after all.

Once I've expended every ounce of energy, I take a seat. And that's when I lose it—the flood of tears come rushing out of me. I can't stop. I feel alone. I feel tired. I feel disconnected. The tools I've used for so long no longer work. And for the first time, I get honest with myself. I hate where I live. I hate the people. I hate the energy. I hate the attitude.

I need to get out.

Without thinking, I pull out my iPhone and hit the big red button. The recording starts. For the next four and a half minutes, I let it flow. I'm detailing where I'm going to be in one year. And for the first time, I can *see* and feel it. It's real. And it's time.

I lay out what's deep inside on the recorder, frame by frame. As the words roll off the tip of my tongue, I'm impressed by how *good* they sound. They feel right. I'm making grand plans to change where I live, start a new business, meet the partner of my dreams, and rediscover the passion that I used to experience daily. I'm outlining my quest in a tantalizing, 4K-resolution picture.

Except there's a problem. Not just any problem: there's a Fort Knox–sized obstacle in the way. I recently signed my name to a five-year lease. Quick math says I'm on the hook for $422,000. Oh yeah, forgot about that. I've got 11 employees. I've got a bricks-and-mortar business. My family is here. Everything I've known and created for the last decade is here. I have no blueprint. I have no prospects. I have no plan.

And yet, I believe. Somehow, someway, it's going to happen. It has to, right?

The Edge Is Your Invitation

What I experienced that night was the *edge*. The edge is the place where the hair on the back of your neck stands up. In a split second, you've achieved a level of clarity unlike any other. You know *exactly* what you must do. There are no excuses, and there's no space for anything except unapologetic belief. The edge engulfs every part of who you are.

And then it's *gone*. Only a few moments later, what was once clarity is now confusion. What was an uplifting life force is now a prison cell. What felt limitless now feels risky. What once felt possible is now a fantasy.

What is *your* edge? Own it and reap the rewards—or watch it disappear. Inspiration is quickly replaced by worst-case scenarios. Possibility is traded for avoiding the unknown. Belief is swapped for the reason you can't do it. Potential is transformed into "being realistic." *A moment of radical insight is shoved into a convenient box labeled "someday."*

The edge is your invitation. It's the launchpad for your quest. This is the moment. Often we hear of life's most defining moments. These usually tend to be *big* life events society has laid out for us: school, college, marriage, career, the birth of a child, a big accomplishment, and so on.

I'd argue that there is no such thing as a defining moment, because if right now is the only moment, then naturally it is the most defining. What I'm really saying here is simple: everything counts.

Especially when you're at your edge.

The Edge Is Daunting, Yet Beautiful

The edge is daunting. You're exposed. You're on the hook, and there's a decision to be made. There's no space to think it through: you do it or you don't.

The edge becomes a bookmark in our lives. The place where we either take one more step into the unknown, betting on ourselves, or run back to safety. It's the place where your heart and head are battling it out in a winner-take-all tug-of-war.

Too many times you've let your head win. The head *loves* to win. It thrives off keeping you comfortable, safe, and stuck. It'd much rather you live a complacent, soul-sucking, safe life than one full of riveting passion created through stepping into the unknown.

Even if that unknown includes a jaw-dropping future or provides you with an opportunity that brings you to your knees (in a great way). The edge is uncomfortable because there are no guarantees on the other side—except the greatest guarantees we could ever have, including:

You won't look back with regret. Regret is heavy. We've all been there. It eats away at our spirit and makes us long for *what could have been.* When you lean into your edge, you'll be able to look back and know you went all in when it counted. This alone provides the inner peace we're so often seeking.

You'll experience wonder and awe. The edge is your threshold, and on the other side is wonder and awe. It's the life force we've always had, designed light up our imagination. In contrast, what's known is boring and zaps our curiosity.

You'll give your life meaning. We're not here for happiness: we're here to have meaningful lives. Lives that matter and are significant. Most importantly—it matters to *us*. Stepping into your edge is how you get there.

You'll have the adventure of a lifetime. Adventure makes us feel alive—and your edge is the ultimate adventure. There's nothing else like it, because you're writing a story about an adventure that most people will only experience through examining the lives of others.

You'll feel immense self-reliance and trust. Self-reliance, as defined by Ralph Waldo Emerson, is the trust we place in ourselves. By leaning into your edge you begin to be able to trust yourself in a world where we've been conditioned to trust others.

You'll be able to tell a riveting story. We all want our life stories to be *worth telling* and worth being remembered for. It's our legacy—what we did during our short time here.

How to Know That You're at Your Edge

Standing at your edge is much like looking out to a distant horizon that separates the world you've known from the world waiting for you. You can feel it, and *this time* it's different. It's unlike anything you've experienced before.

The edge in your life can materialize in countless ways but will include a common set of elements, which will help you to know when you've reached it. These elements include:

You feel a pull. Your edge feels like a magnetic pull—because it is. It's calling on you to grow, to step into a more powerful version of who you are today. When your edge calls you, often you'll find yourself moving toward it with little to no idea as to why.

You're in a painful place. Your edge can come from a place of pain, and that's a great thing. Hear me out: pain is a great motivator, designed to remind you what truly matters.

You can't explain it. Your usual self loves to explain things and figure them out. This is how you stay stuck. In this case, though, logic wins but is also a feedback mechanism to let you know you're getting closer to your edge. You can't explain why, but it's calling you and you *must* go.

It's daunting and beautiful at once. While it's daunting to step closer to your edge, every step builds you. It's beautiful, riveting, and audacious. You feel alive. You feel courageous and bold and have a level of clarity you've never felt before.

If you had no fear, you'd sprint right to it. Your edge is going to come with fear. And that's a great thing—otherwise, it wouldn't be your edge. We must break the conditioned thinking of "If I feel fear, then it means I should back off." No—not here. If you feel it, embrace it.

Arriving at your edge is one thing, but what you do afterward will determine everything. We're not lacking for moments on the edge: what we're lacking is the courage to step into them fully. To stop waiting, or delaying until the date on the calendar moves from 9 to 0 or from 0 to 1. Or until we get the next big promotion or life gets a little *less* hectic. All of these ploys are simply fear masquerading as logic, are simply attempts to make "sense" of something that transcends sense. The leap of your life will come from one place only, and it's *not* your head.

The most important marker of your edge will be the rush you feel through your entire mind, body, and spirit—a combination of intense clarity and knee-buckling fear.

And if you've arrived at your edge by being brought to your knees, that's a good thing.

If Your Edge Brings You to Your Knees, Great

Lisa Nichols felt broken. She desperately needed diapers for her newborn and needed them *bad*. Lisa was 25 years old with her baby's father sitting in Los Angeles County jail—life was looking bleak. She walked to the ATM, punched in the numbers, and prayed. She was attempting to withdraw $20, but the screen glared back at her: insufficient funds.

Must be a mistake, she thought. She tried again, knowing there had to be something in there. And yet, the blue screen came back with the same message. The account balance was $11.42. Living on welfare, Lisa was already struggling.

But this *broke* her. She went home that night and instead of diapers, she wrapped her newborn in towels for two days. The shame and humiliation of standing in line at the welfare office didn't hold a candle to the shame of failing as a mother, of not being able to look into her son's eyes.

This was her *edge*, and it wasn't pretty. That evening she made a vow as her son Jelani:[1]

"Don't you worry, Jelani, Mommy will never, be this broke again." As she said those words, she leaned into her edge. This was different, and she would never be the same after this moment. She explains:

"And that day, what shifted for me, was I was willing...and I don't know if this is going to sound crazy...I was willing to completely die to any form of me that I had been so that I could birth the woman that I was becoming."[2]

If your edge comes from pain, honor it. No, it's not easy—but sometimes, pain is exactly what we need to grab our attention and give us the clarity required to chart a new path and take the leap. Sure, it's messy, and intense—but what's the alternative? If the pain leads to a radical shift and a decision born out of conviction, the on-your-knees moment becomes empowering.

This doesn't mean we're always looking for these moments to become catalysts for change. Psychologists have long researched what compels humans to change and why moments like Lisa's lead to a life-long transformation, and why others stay stuck. In most cases, change is inspired by something we don't want. In others, change is inspired by what we *do* want.

Either way, what matters is that you get to the edge and lean in.

Leap Tip: Avoid the Middle

Bold decisions in life happen at the fringes. Either your circumstances are so dire you can't help but change, or you're being pulled so strongly by a vision of the future that you can't not listen.

Where do dreams die? The middle.

Identify the one place in your life that must change and whether you're going to leverage the pain of staying the same, a vision of the future, or both.

How You Get There Matters Less Than Getting There

Your leap is about a decision. This decision is rooted in conviction, where every part of your body is in alignment. *How* you get there is less important.

Would we rather get there in a state of bliss and inspiration while sipping on our favorite cocktail? Of course, but that's not always the case.

The reality is that our lives will have moments where we take leaps out of sheer pain, recognizing that we never want to experience the same circumstances again. But we'll also have moments where we're in a state of inspiration and are being pulled by a vision we can't *not* bring to life.

Either way, what matters is the result: you were at a place where you chose yourself and committed to a new path. You stepped into the unknown—and reaped incredible rewards.

You're Here for a Reason and It's Time to Unleash It

There are *no* mistakes. You didn't pick up this book for no reason. This life is everything, and you'd better hold onto it with everything you've got. Because putting the leap off for another day, another week, another month, or another year is too much. Every day that passes is a stark reminder of what you *haven't* done, where you lose a fraction of belief. These fractions add up, until one day you're living a life you can't wait to run away from.

If you don't take your leap, it's only going to get *worse*. The voice during your quiet moments will get louder, even though you'll be equipped to drown it out. With every minute that passes, there are missed opportunities for you to step into who you really are.

The stakes have never been higher. And I want you to embrace that, once and for all. This is no time for sugarcoating. It's no time to put things off. You're here, and that's all that matters. That tells me something—the story of who you are and what you want, including:

You're tired of the path you've been on. Belief in a better future drives our sense of fulfillment in this world. It compels us toward powerful decisions and lets us put our head on our pillow at night knowing we're moving toward our dreams. One of the ways of measuring this belief is simply to look one, three, and five years down the path you're currently on and ask the following questions:

When you imagine your future, are you excited and inspired?

Do you see a greater, bolder version of yourself coming to life?

Are hope, possibility, and growth on the horizon?

If the answer to any of these questions is no, that's a great thing. It means you're willing to get honest, which is the first step toward changing anything.

You're tired of feeling stuck in the same place. We've all felt stuck. It's debilitating, and it's a tough pill to swallow. We're pulled by something bigger yet stay in the same place. It impacts every part of our life. We want more, but we simply don't know *how* to get it.

Is there a part of your life where you're feeling stuck and in a rut?

You're tired of thinking bold but not acting bold. Accessing information about business, success, personal development, and living your best life has never been easier. Yet many people seem to be able to regurgitate the principles but don't have much to show for it. You don't want to simply know what it takes to be bold—you're here to *be* bold.

Have you recently gotten excited about the possibility of change and yet woken up a few weeks or months later with nothing to show for it?

You're tired of others around you telling you to "get real." Not everyone is going to "get" your leap and your dreams. Sometimes those closest to you will try to bring you down to keep you safe. Many won't agree about your path, but you must be willing to override their feedback and listen to your own. I'll be giving you some tools that will show you how to use this as leverage instead of being held back.

Do you have a dream, a calling, a vision inside that you've been afraid to let out, or that others have told you isn't worthy?

You've taken a leap in the past but are holding back. You remember taking big leaps in life—maybe you've already launched a business and taken big risks to reap powerful rewards. But now that seems like a distant memory, and you've been putting off another leap that's been calling you.

Have you lost the boldness behind your original leap and lack the courage to step into your next one?

Something is missing, and you don't know what it is. You feel it, you sense it—and it's always in the back of your head. Something is missing, but you don't know *what* to do with this feeling.

Do you get a sense you're not where you should be—yet you don't know how to connect the dots?

If any of those resonated with you, you've come to the right place.

Insight Is Overrated—You Already Know What to Do

You're on your way to accomplishing the first part of any leap: getting honest about where you are today. Don't underestimate the power of this. We've been conditioned to mask (and even blatantly lie about) our edge. We're uncomfortable facing ourselves or even telling the grocery store clerk the truth when he or she asks about our day.

This lack of clarity robs us from the much-needed power to change our circumstances. You may be also be thinking you're here to optimize your life and business and create exponential results. That, too, starts with getting honest. Because no matter how much growth you've experienced, there's always another *leap* waiting for us around the corner. This is the beautiful game of life, the push and pull, the so-called dance between who we are today and who we're becoming.

You already know what to do. This is why insights are cheap and a dime a dozen. But before we get you to a place of identifying the leap of your life, we're going to have to get rid of what's been in the way.

Because something has been holding you back, and the price is the heftiest you could ever pay: your dreams.

Chapter 1 Key Takeaways

- **Your leap is inside of you.** There's a bold step you've been waiting to take, and not taking it is keeping you from not only a deep level of fulfillment but results in your life.

- **The edge is where a decision happens.** Whether it comes from a crumbling moment of pain or an inspiring moment of clarity, only one thing matters: you commit to change.

- **Honor the (real) reason why you're here.** We usually know what to do—yet we pile up reasons why it's not the right time. Identify why you're here and what specifically you're looking for.

CHAPTER 1 LEAP POWER STEP

What is your edge? Identify the big, bold, audacious dream you've been keeping secret *or* a circumstance you know needs to change. Be specific and radically honest.

_____

_____

_____

_____

_____

_____

_____

_____

Notes

1. Goalcast (2017). "Lisa Nichols—Rescue Yourself." https://www.goalcast. com/2017/07/31/lisa-nichols-rescue-yourself. See also Resist Average Academy (n.d.). "The Keys to Abundance and Prosperity with Lisa Nichols." Resist Average Academy, Ep. 98. https://resistaverageacademy.com/98.
2. Lisa Nichols, Inside Quest Interview. https://www.youtube.com/ watch?v=VS5FqBZWpYo

Chapter 2

What's Holding You Back?

Y ou've been holding back. Something has been in the way, because deep down you know there's a leap you haven't taken. Regardless of how much you try to ignore it or drown it out, the feeling that something is missing persists.

They say ignorance is bliss, and sometimes you wish you didn't feel this *longing* for something greater. Then, it would be easier to digest the moments in life passing you by. It may be easier to not feel the impending regret. It would be easier to avoid what's happening under the hood, and how much more time has passed.

I'm going to challenge you to identify where you've been playing small. This part of your story can be used as leverage in pursuit of your dreams. There is nothing wrong with you. You are not broken or defined by your past, no matter how challenging it may have been.

You've simply been held back. These forces at play are influential and keep you at bay, including:

- When you have a powerful insight, they talk you out of it.
- When you're ready to make a big decision, they play private investigator and find the faults.

- When you're ready to lean into the edge of discomfort, they pull the reins back in.

In this chapter, we're going to explore the forces that have been holding you back. We'll explore why these forces are present and the consequences of giving in to them. But we'll also explore how you can use them as *leverage*. You're going to discover how to reframe your relationship with them in a way that serves you, a way that uses them as tools instead of roadblocks, trusted allies, instead of enemies. Otherwise, they'll continue to own you and keep your dreams locked in a safe labeled "someday."

And the great tragedy is that someday may never arrive.

Fear Has Taken Control of Your Life

Fear. We know fear, because we experience it all the time. It's the biggest and baddest of all the negative forces in your life. It's always present underneath the surface and it's relentless and intense. Fear will do anything to keep us at bay.

Fear wants us to be comfortable, play small, and not speak up. Fear loves when we put our dreams off and it talks us into waiting for *tomorrow*. What's one more day? Yeah, tomorrow sounds better, plus it's going to be sunny. *Then*, we'll get started. Except tomorrow, fear is back and has a little more evidence to make you wait, and the cycle repeats itself.

Fear is responsible for most of what you *haven't* done to this point, including:

- Turning your powerful *aha* moment of clarity into nothing but another forgotten memory.
- Robbing you of the emotional, purpose-driven vision you created—and ensuring it stays a fantasy.
- Stopping you from striking up the conversation with a stranger, thereby dissolving the possibility of a once-in-a-lifetime connection.
- Eradicating the clarity around your business launch, and instead telling you to spend more time in research.

- Minimizing your recent win and success into a small feat and finding ways you could have done better.

All of these are damning, with endless consequences. We often forget the domino effect of fear: how a trivial decision not to do something could have led to the opening of a door we never imagined.

However, fear isn't bad. It's actually *awesome*. Hear me out, because fear is powerful and can be used as leverage. What's bad, or rather, toxic, is our *relationship* to fear. Instead of using as the force that it is, we allow it to demolish our hope, keep us stuck, and preventing us from moving forward with our dreams.

Let's examine the conventional wisdom around fear, so you can use it as your compass and use it to supercharge your leap.

#NotesFromTheLeap

Preston Pugmire
Founder, Next Level Life, Speaker

What's the boldest leap you've ever taken and why was this important to you?

I had listened to podcasts for years and always thought "I should do a podcast someday." I leaned on the word *someday* hard because in the back of my mind there was always the fear of "what if no one listens?" Not only did I make the decision to put myself out there and announce that I was going to start a podcast, I told everyone I knew personally and through my social media network that I was going to debut at number 1 in the world in my category. It was uncharted emotional territory for me and it was very uncomfortable.

What did you feel as you made this leap, and what happened after?

There's a scene in *Indiana Jones and the Last Crusade* where Harrison Ford's character stands at a huge ravine inside a cave that is blocking his path. His notebook of secret steps tells him to take a leap of faith. He decides that this means a literal leap, so he closes his eyes, holds his breath, puts his leg out and leans forward into the ravine. At the last moment his foot hits a rock bridge spanning the ravine that was camouflaged making it invisible from his vantage point. This is honestly what it felt like. I had to take a step into the unknown *not* knowing exactly what it would look like or how I would get across my "bridge" to accomplish my goal.

Looking back, what would you tell someone else in a similar circumstance knowing what you now know?

You cannot wait until everything is perfect to decide. I ended up creating an incredible strategy for launching my show and I debuted on iTunes at number 1 in the world in my category of personal development. This has completely changed my life, and now I have a thriving business all coming from the decision to launch the podcast.

Stop Trying to Eradicate Fear

The idea of no fear was a cool lifestyle brand for a while. However, in our quest to eradicate fear, we lose our power and it engulfs us. It's like the pink elephant thought experiment. When we're told to not think of one, guess what? We do.

Although I'm sure the pink elephant you just imagined was awesome, this constant attempt to get rid of a basic part of human evolution that allowed us to get to where we are is fundamentally flawed.

Anyone who's ever given a speech or public talk knows eradicating fear only makes it worse. You focus on it, and then it grows until it paralyzes you. Worse off, because we've attached a negative label to it, we're now ashamed for feeling this way. This cycle repeats itself until we choose to do *nothing*. And when we do nothing, we feel worse. This is Fear 101 becoming a vicious cycle.

But what if there was a way to let go and use fear as a trusted ally?

Release the Conditions

Often, we tend to operate believing the following conditions: if fear is present, it means we shouldn't be doing it. At the very least, it means we should pause, lose all of our momentum, and seek safety.

And so, in life—when fear occurs, it takes a hold of us and stops us cold. This conditional way of living ensures we'll always stay in our comfort zones, we play small, and never speak up. It'll begin to take grip on our day-to-day experience and eradicate our ambition.

It's time to acknowledge fear is there for a reason, and that reason is vitally important with regard to taking the biggest leap of our lives and never looking back.

Pull Up a Seat, Fear Is Here to Stay

The moment you quit your job in a blaze of inspiration and make your first sale, the six-figure launch day, the soulmate connection, or the success you're dreaming of will eradicate fear for good, right?

No, it won't. You better be prepared to extend a warm invitation to fear, because it's here to stay. Often, people will believe that if they just hit *that next outcome*, then fear will be gone.

And then they realize the harsh reality: fear is still there, and sometimes can become even more paralyzing if it hasn't been reframed.

Selling 12 million books, spending four years on the *New York Times* bestseller list, and being named part of the top 100 influential people will jolt you.

And for Elizabeth Gilbert, who'd been writing for various publications on more serious topics, *Eat, Pray, Love* was a not simply a success. It was a napalm bomb explosion of life-altering success that fundamentally shifted every part of her reality.

With this kind of success comes another problem: *dealing* with it. After the wave, Gilbert was faced with the stark realization that her best work, in a commercial sense, was (likely) behind her. This sent her into an existential questioning, down a rabbit hole exploration of unpacking who she really was, a messy endeavor. When you add in fame, you've got a recipe for disaster.

The reality was that success hadn't eradicated her fear; it had simply *shifted* the fear. Once we understand that fear won't go away, we're able to celebrate wins authentically. Furthermore, we won't judge ourselves when we hit the target we dreamed of only to find out there's a new fear we could have never imagined. Let me put this bluntly: *fear in your life is a great thing and shows proof you're on an accelerated path of growth.*

If fear is here to stay, it's time to explore how you can reframe it to use as leverage, clarity, and exponential results in your life.

Reframe 1: Fear Is Your Compass

Your reframe begins by seeking fear regularly. The moment you feel it, you smile. You recognize it. You sense it in your brain, and your body. But instead of running away from it, you lean in. This becomes a daily practice. For example:

- The dread over the tough conversation with your boss becomes a chance for you to learn how to hold tension.
- The uncertainty of the looming business launch becomes the energy required for you to eliminate distraction and tap into your creative genius.
- The fear you feel of pushing yourself physically becomes the needed feedback to sharpen your mental and physical confidence.

Our tendency is to follow the safe path, yet the path leaves us unfulfilled. Fear, then, becomes a trustworthy compass to know you're growing and headed in the right direction (see Figure 2.1).

Reframe 2: Fear Is Your Ally

Once you're paving a new path toward seeking fear, you start to develop an empowering relationship with it. You welcome it, much like you'd welcome someone you respect into your home.

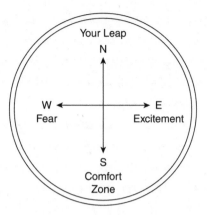

Figure 2.1 Fear is your compass.

This is what being on your edge is supposed to feel like. You recognize the two types of fear. One is the survival instinct, immediate reaction coming from the amygdala. The other is the emotional fear from which you create a worst-case scenario. Both are part of who you are, and building a relationship with these mechanisms allows you to feel empowered.

Now, fear becomes a trusted partner to know exactly *what to do* instead of what not to do. It may not ever become your best friend, and that's okay. But it is a trusted ally and someone you can lean on to make decisions and live your boldest life.

Reframe 3: Fear Is a Prerequisite

Now that you've been able to use fear as a compass and trusted ally, the last part of the reframe puzzle is set.

This is what you've been waiting for, and you'll never miss an opportunity for a life changing moment at the hands of fear again. The last part of the reframe is simple; fear becomes a prerequisite to help make bold decisions. When you feel fear in your life, your comfort zone is being stretched and you have the opportunity to step into your greatness.

I still remember the first time I invested heavily in myself. I'd had a conversation with my mentor about taking a coaching program, and everything in my mind was saying no. Yet, there was something deep within me that recognized this was a do-or-die moment.

With logic screaming in my ear to stop, I took a deep breath and said yes. I was shaking from fear, because the investment was a cool $25,000. When pulling up my bank statement, I had $903 in my checking, and I hadn't paid rent yet. I'd already exhausted most of my account getting there.

But I did it anyway. Susan Jeffers, renowned psychology and author of *Feel the Fear...and Do It Anyway* expands on this topic:[1] "Pushing through fear is less frightening than living with the underlying fear that comes from a feeling of helplessness."

That moment changed my life forever, because investing in the program had nothing to do with *them*. I may as well have written myself a check, because I faced a fear knowing the financial part was the least of my concerns.

What really scared me in that moment was betting on myself, and moving all my chip stacks to the middle of the table in one moment of complete and unapologetic self-trust. Because once you put your dreams on the line, you've got nowhere to hide.

Leap Tip: Run Toward Fear

Flip the script. From here on out, recognize the moments in your life when you *feel* fear, and instead of running from it, lean in. If you weren't experiencing fear, you wouldn't be playing big and bold and stretching your comfort zone.

Identify the last time you felt fear and didn't step up to the plate. Write down five consequences of not taking action.

The Unknown Is Calling, but You're Not Listening

Now that we've reframed fear, it's time to focus on the next pillar holding you back—the unknown. In most people's minds, the unknown is not only uncomfortable, but it's also downright frightening. It's the abyss, the dark cave we all work tirelessly to avoid.

Much like fear, the unknown is responsible for missed opportunities. It's responsible for closing doors that could lead to incredible experiences and saying "no" at the voyage calling us forth. Instead, we seek safety back in the comfort of known—even if that known is painful.

What if we looked at the unknown with a brand-new lens, one that brought excitement and imagination—instead of fear and worst-case scenarios? That's exactly what you'll need when you make your leap. Because the truth is, you don't want to know every single step of your path.

As much as we seek clarity and certainty, we don't want to know the entire story. Think about it. Would you want to know every step of the way on your life's path? No, you wouldn't. We *think* we do sometimes, but we'd lose the essential ingredients of what make this experience special: the mystery, awe, and wonder of not knowing.

So, if you're expecting to know every step of the way in regard to your leap, you've come to the wrong place. Your leap is about writing a story worth reading. And no story is complete without a degree of mystery. Now it's time for you to embrace this mystery in your everyday life.

Leap Tip: Your Greatest Moments

Take a pause and identify the greatest moments of your life. Pick at least two and go back into the way you felt.

Then ask yourself:

- Did I know every step of the path to get there?
- Could I have predicted this moment with precision?
- Was there any uncertainty or fear on the way there?

Once you recognize you've already experienced the ingredients of your leap, you'll shift your awareness and move forward with confidence.

Reframe: The Unknown Is Where the Magic Happens

It's time to change the rules and fall in love with the unknown. Now you're going to perceive the unknown as a place where anything can happen, with the odds stacked in your favor. You're playing with house money, and you *can't* lose. The unknown favors the bold, the daring few who take a chance and trust themselves enough to take the next step.

Much like fear, the reframe will be incomplete without developing a practice of the unknown. Think of these as your training ground, putting in the reps day by day.

Don't overthink it. This is not about a majestic decision to uproot your entire life. This is about trusting the unknown in your day to day.

For example:

- When you're at the grocery store checking out, take the chance to ask the cashier a real question to get to know who that person is.
- When you're driving by the boxing gym and feel compelled to experience it, pull over and go in without doing any research or having prior experience.
- When you're on your way to work and you feel a pull to take the day off with a day trip, make the call to your office because it feels right.

If these seem simple and inconsequential, that's great. It becomes impossible to lean into fear during the high stakes moments of your life without this practice. These moments will add up and help you in stepping into your leap with confidence and power.

But...What Will They Think?

What others may think is holding you back from taking the leap. You may say to yourself, "I don't care what other people think." Yeah, right.

We all care, and we all care way too much. David Foster Wallace sums up this universal feeling brilliantly in his book *Infinite Jest*[2]:

> You will become way less concerned with what other people
> think of you when you realize how seldom they do.

Often, we overestimate how much people care about what we're doing and create constructs in our minds using *them* as reasons to not do what we know is right.

Think about your past 24 hours. Examine some of the choices you made when you felt others were judging you. These happen all the time, often unconsciously. Much like fear and the unknown, they hold you back from fully expressing who you are.

For example:

- You really wanted to take a selfie celebrating your morning work-out, but you didn't want people in the gym to think you're one of *those* people.
- You really wanted to ask a question at the event you were recently at, but you didn't want others to think it was dumb.
- You know you have to launch your business or side hustle, but you're worried about your co-workers finding you on social media.

It's time to release the way you and I experience judgment, once and for all.

No Matter What, You Will Be Judged

Here's the secret? **No matter what you do in life, you're going to be judged.** You can stay stuck the rest of your life, and you'll be judged. You can take the bold leap, and you'll be judged. If you speak up, you'll be judged. If you stay quiet, you'll be judged. It's part of life, and it's never going to go away. Once you recognize this, the stranglehold judgment has on you will begin to loosen.

However, there is one judgment that matters: it's the judgment from the person looking back at you in the mirror every single day. That *does* carry weight, because we have to live with ourselves every single day. We take ourselves everywhere.

If we avoid the leap, we must live with the fact that we're going to judge ourselves the rest of our lives for *not* making the decision we knew was right. Yes, we can rationalize and compartmentalize it as much as we want. But it won't go away.

Often, time only makes it worse.

Reframe: Judgment Is a Mirror

It's time to reframe judgment. It starts with recognizing that when people judge you, it's never about you. This realization is liberating. For example:

- If people are ripping the author with personal attacks on Twitter, it isn't because they have something constructive to say but, rather, because it's easier to attack than to offer constructive criticism or create something of their own.

  Secret: They're dying to create something, and you triggered what they haven't done.
- If people are making one-off remarks during the meeting when you spoke up, it's because deep down, they wanted to contribute.

  Secret: They want to be heard and went against their own call to speak up.
- If people on social media are making passive-aggressive remarks when you celebrate something, it's because they're feeling inferior to you.

  Secret: They know there's success out there for them, and they're frustrated.

Understanding this allows you to dissolve the emotional impact of judgment and continue to take the next step forward.

You Don't Believe It's Possible for You

Deep down, you don't believe your leap is possible for you. Often, I'll tell stories about those who have taken life-altering leaps, and someone will say:

"Well, they had connections, so *of course* it worked out."

"They're disciplined and that's why they experienced success."

"They were at the *right* place at the right time. I can't repeat that."

Facepalm. All these are mechanisms for the same thing: letting ourselves off the hook by glorifying someone else's traits. The truth is, they're not unique or special. The people you look up to are the same as you and me. They wake up with the same doubts, insecurities, feelings of unworthiness, and frustrations as you do. They're on the verge of throwing up before they hop on stage. They feel overwhelmed, and like there's not enough time. They want to give up and give in long before they accomplish their dreams.

Remember, those you look up to are not special or flying on some magical carpet. They're human. They experience the same trials and tribulations you do. However, it's what happens next that changes the course of a life. The great separator, then, is what they do after the voices of doubt rise to the surface. And the backbone of it all is *belief.*

You're Unwilling to Swim in Discomfort

Your leap is going to require you to get *dirty.* It's going to require you to get messy and wrestle with a myriad of emotions. One of the main obstacles in people's way is their unwillingness to be uncomfortable. They say they want the result of the leap, but they're not willing to do the work of the leap.

We're conditioned to avoid discomfort at a young age. We place it in a box labeled *bad* and avoid at all costs. Yet, I'm here to tell you the quality of your life will be dependent on how often and to what degree you're willing to get uncomfortable.

Sound crazy? Hear me out. Through discomfort we learn about ourselves. It's where we're able to give an experience meaning. And most importantly, it's where fulfillment occurs, not in a one-shot dopamine hit of happiness.

We can manufacture a one-shot hit of happiness right now—sex, ice cream, and the biggest double-patty order from Carl's Jr.'s will make us happy for a bit. But it's fleeting, and when it fades, we're worse than when we started.

By facing yourself day after day, with a willingness to get messy, that's a direct route to fulfillment. Your leap is all about getting uncomfortable, and if you're unwilling to face it, or operate under the illusion that it's going to be sunshine, puppies, and butterflies, you're playing the wrong game.

You Only Believe When It's Convenient

Belief is binary. There is no in-between, there is no halfway, there is no 79%. You're in or you're out. You can't believe 50% and then increase 5% every time you experience a win. Because if you're not 100% in, you're out of alignment and everyone can feel it. The marketplace feels it, the people you interact with feel it, and worst of all, you feel it.

So, what's stopping you from 100%? We've already covered the common suspects: fear, the unknown, judgment, or a mix of all three. Often, we believe conditionally, that is, when I see proof of my outcome coming true, then I'll believe.

It doesn't work this way, and you know it. You must believe first. We'll explore belief deeper in Chapter 8, but for now I'll leave you with this quotation from Stuart Chase:

> "For those who believe, no proof is necessary. For those who don't believe, no proof is possible."[3]

Now that we've identified the most common forces standing in the way between you and a life you can't wait to wake up for, it's time to explore the biggest price we pay for not taking our leap: a life unlived.

Chapter 2 Key Takeaways

- **Fear is always part of your leap; it's how you use it.** Reframing your relationship with fear is the first step: if fear wasn't there, you wouldn't be thinking boldly enough.
- **The unknown is where the magic happens.** The greatest moments of our lives happen in the unknown. Instead of looking at it from a place of worst-case scenario, flip the script and embrace the place where anything can happen.
- **Judgment is part of life, no matter what you do.** Whether you play small for the approval of others or live out loud, someone will judge you. The question is will you judge yourself?

CHAPTER 2 LEAP POWER STEP

What is holding you back? Without spending too much time analyzing, identify five reasons you're being held back. Putting them on paper allows you to step back and see them for what they really are.

_____

_____

_____

_____

_____

_____

Notes

1. www.susanjeffers.com/home/detailtemplate.cfm?catID=2234.

2. https://www.goodreads.com/quotes/385500-you-will-become-way-less-concerned-with-what-other-people.

3. https://spartacus-educational.com/USAchaseS.htm.

Chapter 3

Life, Unlived

In the personal development, do-these-seven-things-to-ensure-your-success world, there's endless chatter around morning routines. You can't spend any time online perusing a blog in this world without mentioning these routines, or the countless books that have sprung from them.

I say these things, too. No doubt there is an incredible power in setting the tone for your day with clarity, energy, space, and rituals to put you in a peak emotional state. However, one of the most powerful morning routines I have has nothing to do with gratitude or aligning my chakras.

It's reading Reddit. Often considered the garbage bin of the Internet along with Twitter, reading Reddit is a crucial part of my morning routine.

The truth is, I'd be *lost* without it. I'd forget to live with purpose. I'd fall prey to the little details trying to pull me away from my vision—gossip, what someone posted on Instagram or how my bulldog still can't follow through on a "paw" request.

I don't simply read Reddit aimlessly, I read one *specific* post.[1] In fact, aside from this one post, I know very little about Reddit and spend no other time on it.

The post I read every single morning is shown in Figure 3.1.[2]

TIFU my whole life. My regrets as a 46 year old, and advice to others at a crossroad

TIFU. More like more whole life really.

Hi, I, my name's John. I've been lurking for a while, but I've finally made an account to post this. I need to get my life off my chest. About me. I'm a 46 year old banker and I have been living my whole life the opposite of how I wanted. All my dreams, my passion, gone. In a steady 9-7 job. 6 days a week. For 26 years. I repeatedly chose the safe path for everything, which eventually changed who I was.

Today I found out my wife has been cheating on me for the last 10 years. My son feels nothing for me. I realised I missed my father's funeral FOR NOTHING. I didn't complete my novel, travelling the world, helping the homeless. All these things I thought I knew to be a certainty about myself when i was in my late teens and early twenties. If my younger self had met me today, I would have punched myself in the face. I'll get to how those dreams were crushed soon.

Let's start with a description of me when I was 20. It seemed only yesterday when I was sure I was going to change the world. People loved me, and I loved people. I was innovative, creative, spontaneous risk-taking and great with people. I had two dreams. The first, was writing a utopic/dystopic book. The second, was travelling the world and helping the poor and homeless. I had been dating my wife for four years by then. Young love. She loved my spontaneity, my energy, my ability to make people laugh and feel loved. I knew my book was going to change the world. I would show the perspective of the 'bad' and the 'twisted', showing my viewers that everybody thinks differently, that people never think what the do is wrong. I was 70 pages through when I was 20. I am still 70 pages in, at 46. By 20, I had backpacking around New Zealand and the Phillipines. I planned to do all of Asia, then Europe, then America (I live in Australia by the way). To date, I have only been to New Zealand and the Phillipines.

Now, we get to where it all went wrong. My biggest regrets. I was 20. I was the only child. I needed to be stable. I needed to take that graduate job, which would dictate my whole life. To devote my entire life in a 9-7 job. What was I thinking? How could I live, when the job was my life? After coming home, I would eat dinner, prepare my work for the following day, and sleep at 10pm, to wake up at 6am the following day. God, I can't remember the last time I've made love to my wife.

Figure 3.1   My favorite "Today I F★★★★d Up" post on Reddit.

Ouch. There isn't a time when I've read this text and not experienced a sinking feeling in my gut, and if you did too, *great.* This text hits me hard. Bourbon, neat, to the face, hard; sparring with a UFC champion, hard; 41 degree-ice-bath hard. It hits me harder than the thousands of books I've read in other disciplines. And it hits me this way because it's real. I can feel the emotion of regret in every word and the heaviness it comes with. Within these words, I learn the most valuable lesson:

The pain of regret will destroy our lives. It is the life we didn't live. It's the mundane existence that comes from it. I could tell you what it is, but you've just felt it by reading about John in Figure 3.1. We've all felt

John's pain in our own lives, at least to some degree. The unlived life is an easy trap we can all slide into. It's a hollow existence and feels like something is always missing. Worse, you feel like it's simply too late and the window has *closed*. This is the path where hopelessness is the only option.

Regret doesn't discriminate. You can achieve all the external markers of success—the bank account, the cars, and even the relationships. Sometimes, these make everything worse. An unlived life is exactly what it sounds like—being alive in this experience called life, but not truly living it. You get to a place where you're resigned, apathetic, and believe it's too late. You missed your shot. And now it's over, so what's the point?

Now, if I were to spend time with John, I'd tell him it's *not* too late. In fact, this post made the rounds on Reddit with over 4,000 comments and he received endless support to get back on track, finish the book, and repair the relationship with his son. I'm hoping he made that choice because while life does have windows of opportunity, they don't fully close shut until we're gone.

In this chapter, we're going to go deep on what it means to experience an unlived life. We'll explore the *real* price you're paying for not taking your leap, and why it holds the keys to ensuring you don't experience the heaviness of regret or thinking it's too late for you.

Leap Tip: (Reverse) Visualization

You've heard of visualization for success, but what about *reverse* visualization? Instead of your dreams, I want you to amplify the pain of the future if you stay in the same place. If you choose to *not* grow, and to play small.

What does life look and feel like five years down the line? Don't stop until it hurts, and play out the worst-case scenarios.

The Greatest Price You'll Ever Pay

Bonnie Ware spent a significant amount of time in deep conversation with people who were dying during their last days. She stumbled upon this career by accident, yet her compassion kept her in it. She also knew she was experiencing the highest level of wisdom one could ever receive: from those who had *nothing* to hide.

They were naked. Sometimes literally, but mostly naked in the sense they were sitting at death's door. Some would go on to last a year, some a couple months or as little as a few days.

Honesty and truth were at the core of what they'd pass to her—with none of the filters so many of us tend to use. She'd engage in these conversations, and then the person she was caring for would pass. She'd have a heavy heart and remember their gems. And the cycle would repeat itself.

What Bonnie learned was compiled, posted online, and it went viral. Resonating with people of all backgrounds, her content became a book and a platform. She possessed a level of raw wisdom few achieve until older age, and she needed to share it with the world. The number-one regret she identified in her conversations was simple:

"I wish I'd had the courage to live a life true to myself, not the life others expected of me."[3]

This is the ultimate price you pay for not taking your leap. It's heavy, and it hurts. There is nothing more heartbreaking than getting to the end of our experience here and coming to the stark realization we *didn't* do it.

We didn't push the chips to the middle of the table when we had our shot. We didn't go all in when we had the chance. We didn't say what needed to be said, and we didn't pursue the path calling us forward. We didn't listen to ourselves, and instead followed the external voices telling us what we should do. Not because we wanted it, but because we knew it'd make others approve of us.

Although this price is a heavy burden to pay during your last days, at that point, there's not much left to do. What's even more painful is living with this day in and day out, and you've likely experienced it. Life seems to be lacking color and there's a stubborn voice in the back of your head reminding you of what's been missed.

Every day that passes, is a reminder. Time does little to help and even adds to the frustration. You've been there, and you may even be there right now. If so, *great*. Because you still have time to chart a new path, make a bold decision and choose something different. No matter how off course you may have been, there's always an opportunity for a detour and course correction.

Understanding Regret

Regret is an emotion we experience daily. A 1984 study revealed regret was the second most frequently experienced emotion behind love. Defined clinically, regret is simply "a negative emotion predicated on an upward, self-focused, counterfactual inference."[4]

I know, you have no idea what it means. Put simply, regret is the feeling expressed by John in Figure 3.1—wondering how a different choice or decision in our lives could had led to a greater result. Psychologists call these "alternative histories," and the imagined futures they generate, "counterfactual thoughts."[5]

We've all experienced these firsthand. The missed opportunity in talking to the stranger at the event, the chance we had to launch the business—the time we knew we had to act yet chose to wait.

But the thing that makes regret much worse are the tapes we replay in our heads on what could have been.

What Makes Regret Much, Much Worse

It's one thing to experience regret in life, but it's another to obsess over the endless scenarios on where we fell short. This process, labeled rumination, is considered the worst part of regret. People who can't let go and let their past keep them stuck right now are ruminators. So is the friend who mentions the same exact business deal or relationship gone wrong from a decade ago. It's the co-worker who's *still* agitated at what he or she didn't say to their boss last quarter.

Dr. Amy Summerville knows a little something about regret. She runs The Regret Lab at Miami University where she studies all forms of regret and its impact on human behavior—past, present, and future.

She expands on this topic of rumination:

> ...what we found is that people who have ruminative
> regrets—so that they're both having this regret, but also
> having it be something that's intrusive and repeated—tend
> to be people who are also experiencing the *most* negative
> outcomes, so are more likely to have clinical depression
> symptoms, anxiety symptoms, things like that.[6]

Rumination made Bronnie Ware's patients reflect back and identify their lifelong regrets. Meaning, they'd have regret over a part of
their life they didn't take a chance on, or where they played it safe.

Once life began to slow down with advanced age and health issues,
they had more idle time to reflect and bring these regrets to the surface. Instead of looking back with a wide smile, they looked back with
more disgust than awe.

Leap Tip: Visit Your Local Cemetery

When faced with your mortality, you remember what's real. You focus
on the essential, and the day-to-day problems dissolve.

One of the most powerful practices you can do is visit your local
cemetery once a month. Treat it as the powerful wakeup call it is; you,
too, will be there soon.

How do you want to be remembered? Often, our mortality is something we avoid—and yet, it contains the reminder we need to live right
now. As Steve Jobs once famously said,

> Remembering that you're going to die is the best way to avoid the
> trap of thinking you have something to lose. You are already naked.
> There is no reason not to follow your heart.[7]

You Will Regret What You Didn't Do

Flash back to the biggest regrets of your life. Where do they come
from? For most people, they don't come from what has been done.
They come from what hasn't been done, and *what could have been*. Even

if the action you took was considered a mistake, it usually involves less regret as time passes, because there's no element of mystery, and we can often find a silver lining within the mistake. We can tell ourselves "at least we went for it." We can extract a *win*: a lesson from the experience, trusting ourselves or simply finding a new opportunity that was otherwise not available earlier.

To summarize: **there is no loss in going for *it***. There are countless coping mechanisms we use to soothe the discomfort of regret, with one being the thought that there's always another chance.

Although this can be psychologically healthy and give us *hope*, sometimes, it simply isn't true, and the opportunity is gone for good. A 2017 study, *The Ideal Road Not Taken*,[8] expands:

> In contrast, "undoing" a failure to act is often impossible. The one who got away may now be married to someone else; some talents can only be fully developed if one starts young; a once-in-a-lifetime job opportunity comes around only once.[9]

When you feel the pull to do it now, don't wait, or else you may miss your window.

#NotesFromTheLeap

Jay Nixon
Owner, Thrive Fitness and Author

What's the boldest leap you've ever taken and why was this important to you?

I left corporate America and start living my life instead of merely existing to fulfill someone else's dreams. No money, no clients, no ten-year plan. Just an unwavering belief in myself and a sincere desire to help people. At the time, I just existed. My life wasn't purposeful, profitable, or passionate. I knew I couldn't live the next 70 years that way.

What did you feel as you made this leap, and what happened after?

Extreme uncertainty [was] followed by the biggest adrenaline rush you could ever imagine. I would assume this is what someone that does drugs feels like (I've never done a drug in my life, I know I'm super boring). On the other side I found true wealth. Not just money, but [in] all areas of my life: Health, Relationships, Money and Spirituality. What I've been able to create is truly that, it has given me wealth both in the tangible and metaphorical sense.

Looking back, what would you tell someone else in a similar circumstance knowing what you now know?

You can be, do, and have everything you desire if you are willing to make the decision that you will take obsessive action on your goals everyday—and most importantly on the day you don't feel like it.

Don't Miss Your Window

We have windows of opportunity in life, snapshots in time when a door opens. These moments are designed to take us on the ride of a lifetime. During these junctures, we have fingerprint-specific combinations of life experience and timing that can't be replicated.

Often, we let those moments pass. We tell ourselves we'll have another chance. There's always tomorrow. We let ourselves off the hook and package up logic disguised as fear.

But what if we're *wrong?* What if we had that *one* moment when everything changed? What if there'll never be another chance like that again? For me, I recognized I had a window a few years ago. That window lasted all of 15 seconds.

It was a random Tuesday afternoon in early January, and I desperately needed a Wi-Fi connection. An urgent business email was pending, and a few thousand dollars were at stake. I was in a rush, and as I flew down the highway, I remembered there was a Starbucks around the corner.

Rushing out of my car like a madman, I walked feverishly with my head down; I was a man on a mission. Wi-Fi was *all* mine.

And that's when I saw her. Striking, beautiful and with an energy that seemed to pull me. It was 1:13 p.m.on a random Tuesday. She was crossing the street. I had to find Wi-Fi. I wouldn't even know what to say. My mind was scattered. I can't be distracted.

Next thing I know, we're having a conversation. We spoke for a few minutes, had a mutual connection, and exchanged contact information. On a random day and time, crossing a 15-second crosswalk—both our lives changed forever. Fifteen seconds on either side, and the opportunity would have been either painfully awkward or simply missed.

I never planned I'd meet my fiancée that way. I thought I'd meet her at an event, or through a mutual relationship, yet it was perfect. I had a window, and a tight one at that. Facing rejection, awkwardness, or some random guy interrupting her daydream, I did it *anyway*. This is the power of recognizing the window as it happens.

Now, let's paint a different outcome if I had stayed committed to Wi-Fi and ignored the pull I felt when I saw her. The Wi-Fi, in this case, represented my logical self. It's a responsibility. So, it would have become easy and convenient for me to rationalize the window I had missed by saying: "She was probably busy, not single—and oh, yeah, I really needed this money."

Truth be told, it would have been easy to talk myself into this. After all, it was partially *true*. I did need the money. Thinking she was not single was fear taking over and winning.

But something deeper would have been eating away at me, and that represents the *ideal* self. The part of me that knew this interaction could be special, otherwise I wouldn't have been energetically pulled. Maybe she *was* single. Maybe she *was* open. Maybe because of one 4-minute conversation, my life would never be the same.

This is the price to pay for missing our windows in life. But the only reason I was able to step into the opportunity that day and risk rejection was because of I was able to use past regret as leverage.

And you can do the same.

Using Regret as Leverage

Despite all the downer talk on regret, it's not all bad. In fact, it's the most *hopeful* emotion from the batch of commonly experienced negative ones. Because it's not whether you and I will experience regret. What separates regret from becoming hopeful versus hopeless, debilitating versus empowering is simple: what we do *next*.

In a study performed by psychologists at the University of Illinois in 2008, researchers found regret to be the most beneficial out of the 12 identified "negative" traits including anger, anxiety, boredom, disappointment, disgust, fear, frustration, guilt, jealousy, sadness, and shame.[10] **If we process it correctly, regret can be used as leverage to make bigger and bolder decisions in the future.** We can use our experience of past regrets to ensure they don't happen again.

And that's exactly what I did on that January day. I'd let other potential opportunities slip through my fingers. I'd talked myself out of social circumstances. I'd told myself stories that it was simply not the right time, and I'd have another shot. We do this in all areas of life, and it comes up with my clients in business all the time.

For months, I'd been working with an entrepreneur looking to scale their service-based business. When working together, we identified an obvious roadblock: there were a few bad employees bringing the entire team down.

I don't make decisions for my clients, but I create the container and perspective for them to make decisions. And in this case, it was obvious. It was time to get rid of these employees. The time was up. The show was over. It was all crystal clear.

Except my client didn't do it. He knew what he had to do, and he had a window. He kept talking himself out of it:

"Well, it's busy season in the business—so I'll do it *after*."
"Some days, they're actually decent. Plus, no one else can do their job."

"It's too hard to find someone else."

We've all played this game, and then a few months down the line during the busiest time of the year, they bolted without saying a word. They simply didn't show up. My client was devastated with them deciding to leave *him*.

During our next session, he was experiencing massive regret with not taking swift action. But instead of ruminating on where he fell short, we used it as leverage. He would never again *wait* to make a hiring or firing decision. Using a trusting-your-gut mechanism we'll explore later, he'd make the decision then and there.

Regret gives us **an opportunity to choose something differ-ent.** If you can flip the script on your regrets, they become a way to supercharge your future. And most important, with the right perspective they can be seen as something worth having experienced. Dr. Summerville expands:

"Regret is actually a very *hopeful* emotion. It's something that is helping us learn from our mistakes and do better in the future."[11]

If you're reading this and have regrets, welcome to life. The question isn't whether you have some; it's what you are going to do with yours.

Flip the Script and Choose Something New

Now that we've explored what an unlived life looks and feels like, with the underlying theme of regret, it's time to flip the script. It's time to put this into action and put you in a place of clarity moving forward.

I want you to take a moment and identify your biggest regret to date. The opportunity that passed you by, getting anchored in an environment you hated or staying in that relationship for two years *too* long.

We all have them, and I want you to go there. Often, we use a cop-ing mechanism for regret in the form of avoidance. It's easier to ignore the *pain* of a regret than to face it head on. However, by not facing it we lose the power to make a new choice.

Before you read on, I want you to identify that *one* regret that you haven't dealt with. And I'm encouraging you to sit with that feeling. Let it engulf you and remind you of not knowing what could have been.

Often, I use the phrase, *it's the not knowing that kills you.* And with regret, that couldn't be more spot on. With your regret in mind, I want you to take a moment and ask yourself a few questions. Remember, this isn't about judging yourself. Rather, it's a way to face the regret and use it as leverage for the *leap* of your life:

- When you think of this regret, what exactly do you feel? Be specific.
- What did your ideal self *really* want to do in that moment? Be specific.
- What specifically held you back? Describe the prevailing narrative or excuse you used.
- What is it about this moment or regret that you don't want to feel in the future?
- Now that it's happened, take a moment and identify at least three positives from experiencing this regret to help you in the future.

Using this process, you'll be able to not only release the rumination associated with regret but also flip the script and use it as leverage next time. You'll face another similar circumstance and that time you'll choose something different. You'll know, regardless of outcome, you won't experience regret again.

There Is No Loss in Going for It

The only loss is the enduring pain that is felt when you don't go for it. In other words, you're playing with *house money* when you push the chips to the table and go all in. John's story is one of countless stories, and the unlived life is as available to us as it was to him.

Your leap is the path to ensure you don't wake up with a life in which you didn't truly live, a life in which you kept your gifts to yourself and woke up one day wondering where it all went wrong.

Leap Tip: Really, What's the Worst-Case Scenario?

If you're here, it's because you want *something* to change. Often, we'll cling on to a painful reality and not take our leap in fear of losing it.

Remember: there is always another unfulfilling job, an environment you hate, and a relationship you can't wait to get away from.

Make a list of the worst-case scenarios. Once you get them out of your head and on paper, they lose their power over you.

When Felix Baumgartner, the world-famous skydiver, stood at the edge of space, the world tuned in because it was a high stakes moment full of risk. He was breaking the limits of human potential.

But was it actually *risky?* It depends who you ask. For Felix, it wasn't risky at all. For those in the program, it wasn't either. For countless viewers and the world watching, it may have well been one of the riskiest endeavors they had ever seen.

And therein lies the lesson: risk is subjective, and the greatest risk you'll ever face is *not* going for it.

It's time to redefine risk, once and for all.

Chapter 3 Key Takeaways

- Regret can be a roadblock or a catalyst. You can use regret as leverage to make new decisions or stay stuck thinking *what could have been*. Which will you choose?

- Don't miss your window. In life, we have windows of opportunity. Often, we talk ourselves out of them, saying they'll come back. Instead, recognize our lives can change in an instant and don't miss your windows.

- There is no loss in going for it. We regret what we *didn't* do. Even if you swing and miss, you tap into a powerful emotional state knowing you took a chance.

CHAPTER 3 LEAP POWER STEP

Complete the biggest-regret exercise below. Take yourself to the moment of greatest regret, and think about what followed. Immerse yourself in these feelings. Now, how can this help you make bolder decisions today?

_____

_____

_____

_____

_____

_____

Notes

1. To read the full post: https://old.reddit.com/r/tifu/comments/2livoo/tifu_my _whole_life_my_regrets_as_a_46_year_old/?st=jng6aj3s&sh=b9ec25ed.

2. https://livelearnevolve.com/man-reveals-how-choosing-comfort-in-his-20s -led-to-a-life-of-emptiness-and-pain/.

3. https://bronnieware.com/blog/regrets-of-the-dying/.

4. https://www.ncbi.nlm.nih.gov/pmc/articles/PMC2394712/.

5. http://smagazineofficial.com/living/science-of-regret-06137336.

6. https://www.npr.org/templates/transcript/transcript.php?storyId =550260750.

7. https://news.stanford.edu/2005/06/14/jobs-061505/.

8. http://psycnet.apa.org/record/2017-21180-001.

9. http://psycnet.apa.org/record/1998-12057-002.

10. https://www.ncbi.nlm.nih.gov/pmc/articles/PMC2413060/.

11. https://www.npr.org/templates/transcript/transcript.php?storyId =550260750.

Chapter 4

Risk, Redefined

G iordano Bruno was as unconventional as they come. He was a sixteenth-century Italian philosopher, and a man of innumerable interests. Cosmology, science, studying the universe and even magic—Bruno spent a large part of his life running from authorities and conducting lectures of what he believed to be true.

His core thesis, written in 1584, entitled *On the Infinite Universe and Worlds* argued if there is one of these worlds, then there are infinite numbers of planets and stars in the Universe. Today, this seems obvious. In his time, however, there were severe consequences to pay, and he spent most of his time on the run.

But he didn't care. In contrast to Copernicus, who delayed the publishing of his works by 40 years for what many say was fear of retaliation, imprisonment, or death, Bruno was boisterous around his beliefs. He was loud, and a trailblazer.

On a return trip home from England to Italy to print his works, Bruno was captured and spent nine years in prison as he awaited trial.

But he was given an out: recant his beliefs and lectures, and he'd be saved. If not, he'd be burned at the stake at the hands of the inquisition. Many of Bruno's contemporaries had chosen to retract their teachings in the face of death.

But Bruno remained committed, and when the sentence finally arrived on eight counts of heresy, Bruno proclaimed: *"Perhaps you, my judges, pronounce this sentence upon me with greater fear than I receive it."*[1]

At the time, Bruno was seen as a martyr and treated as such. And yet in the face of death, he took the biggest gamble knowing very well the outcome was the loss of life. On the surface, it's easy to proclaim Bruno took an *absurd* risk.

Or did he?

Face the Music: Life Is Already Risky

Life is already risky. Let's remind ourselves that we're currently spinning at 1,037 miles per hour while orbiting a massive star that is going at another 67,000 miles per hour. And that star is part of a larger galaxy, the Milky Way—which is also moving at a brisk 1.3 million miles per hour.

Enough with the science, but I'm painting you the picture that life is risky. We're here, we're alive. Safety is simply an illusion. We haven't even addressed the fact we're being kept alive by a fist-sized muscle in our left chest that acts on electrical impulses pumping up to 2,000 gallons a day.

The fact that you're here is a miracle. When we think about the bigger picture, the small stuff tends to consume us *less*. We're able to make faster decisions and flip the script on how we perceive risk – and use risk to pursue our leap. In light of this:

Quitting the soul-sucking job you've been stuck at for six years seems *less* risky.

Making the move out from the toxic environment you live in doesn't seem as big as a deal.

Stepping into the tough conversation you've been avoiding, which has been consuming your thoughts, now seems like a no brainer.

Hiring your first employee when you're strapped for cash seems like less of a big deal.

This is the power of redefining risk and playing the game by your own rules. With each step, you start to craft the life of your dreams. Not the one someone else wants for you, but the one *you* want. And that energy changes everything.

Because the truth is simple: **the way you and I have been told to perceive risk is flawed and is holding us back from living our best life.**

Until now, that is.

Risk Is a Liar

From the time we're brought into this world, we're fed a narrative about risk and the way we perceive it. We're told it's better to be safe than sorry. Play it safe, and we'll be rewarded. Don't be too loud or dream too big. Don't stand out, or else you're going to offend others.

It's not working. At least not in the way I define *working*. It's not working for you either, unless your definition of success involves a predictable, safe, and mundane future. But you're here, which means you're wanting to live a life on your terms. For far too long, we've looked at standing out as being risky, and we're paying a hefty price.

But what if the real risk was fitting in, to seek the approval at the expense of our own?

Risk Is in the Eye of the Beholder

Risk is an entirely subjective experience. We know this, and we experience this every day in our lives. On a moment-to-moment basis, we're assessing risk and allowing it to impact our decision-making. From the trivial to the life changing decisions, risk is always present in the back of our minds.

However, we rarely assess whether the way we tolerate and take on risk is actually *working*. We often let our risk-taking mechanisms run in the background while we experience life, even if we're feeling stuck or compelled to something greater.

In having thousands of conversations with those who have not only achieved massive success but also made bold decisions in the face of fear, I've identified three core pillars required to make risk work for *us*, not against us.

But before I share those pillars, we must understand what we're already playing with.

You're Designed to Be Risk Averse

You and I are designed to be risk averse, because our lives might depend and have depended on this mechanism. Thousands of years ago, we needed to treat every noise as a potential threat, and there was no time to consider the upside of a ruffling noise in the woods. We needed to live.

This has stayed with us, and now that there's zero possibility of a tiger eating us on the way to lunch, we must override this mechanism. Universally, we operate with an intense degree of negativity bias, which simply means that given the same amount of information, we're hardwired to be more emotionally charged (and thus, focused) on what could go wrong. The amygdala, an almond shaped mass inside the brain is responsible for decoding our emotions and helping us make fast decisions. However, two-thirds of the neurons inside our amygdala are wired for negativity.

Without stepping too much into brain science, it's crucial to understand that our operating system is rooted in fear. And by listening to this primal part of the brain, we can miss out on life's biggest opportunities.

Of course, one of those is the leap of your life.

No Risk, No Magic, No Riveting Story

The great tragedy of not redefining risk to serve your dreams and aspirations is you'll always wonder *what if*. Without reframing risk and ditching the safe path in life, you'll be unable to write the life story that you know is deep within you. The riveting tale, the page-turner you can't put down will instead become another predictable book.

That's not you. It's not why you're here.

On many days, I can be overheard talking about opportunity cost in my downtown Phoenix office with my clients. It happens so often, it must sound like I'm teaching economics. But understanding opportunity cost is crucial to the success of your leap and making the right decision, at the right time.

Opportunity cost is at the core of all our decision-making and can be summed easily: it's what you give up in order to get something. It's the difference between what you choose now and the next best alternative. Whether that's choosing to eat pizza instead of going to the gym or choosing to stay at your current job—there's *always* a price to pay.

For example, Steve is working a corporate gig and he's making $85,000 a year—what psychologists have found to be the sweet spot for happiness and fulfillment. He's tired of it though, it's been eating away at his soul. He can't deal with his boss. He has a passion and purpose much greater but has found himself stuck.

The opportunity cost, what Steve's trading in right now for what *could* be is the following:

- **Financial prosperity.** If Steve stays at his corporate gig, the *best-*case scenario is a 5% increase in salary every year.
- **Purposeful work and fulfillment**. By staying on the same path, Steve is trading away his own personal fulfillment and emotional health.
- **Health, energy, and vitality.** Steve's lack of connection to his work is crushing his health, and he's constantly feeling exhausted, having to say no to things he really wants to do (hiking, mountain biking, adventures).
- **Relationship growth.** Steve's wife Emily feels her husband's dissatisfaction. She's felt it for a while now and done her best to support him. But they're missing the spark, because *he's* missing the spark.

So, is this worth $85,000? It depends on who you ask. Often, people will say yes until it gets so bad they can't not change. Or, they wake up one day to a pink slip to realize the truth all along: no employer is loyal to any employee.

Now, let's redefine risk so it works for you once and for all by examining the three risk pillars.

Risk Pillar 1: Clarity Around Your Purpose

The first step to redefining risk in your life is to have clarity around a bolder purpose or mission. Without this, there's minimal chance you will make bold decisions in the face of risk. Having a driving force, which we'll explore in Part II, Before Your Journey, is crucial to the success of your leap.

Your vision will dramatically shift the way you perceive risk on the way to carving out your path. It must be powerful, and it must compel you in a way that's bigger than simply yourself. Felix Baumgartner had a vision and mission to redefine the limits on human performance, and although he had his personal vision attached to it, it wasn't *only* about himself.

You must have a bold vision, otherwise you'll get stuck in the day to day and make decisions designed to keep you anchored to your past, instead of propelled like wildfire into your future.

Risk Pillar 2: Playing the Long Game

Paulo Coehlo's second book, *The Alchemist*, was published by a small Brazilian publisher and slotted for 900 copies. His publisher said it would never sell that many, and he was right. Coelho was dropped, and at 41 years old with no signs of success, the safe path was to quit.

But he didn't, because he was playing the long game. At 41, most would say the long game was over, but he was barely getting started. The rest, of course, is history, and *The Alchemist* is one of the most successful and enduring works of all time with over 65 million copies sold to date.[2]

In a world where instant gratification and this-must-work-now pressure is the norm, playing the long game allows you to take more risks.

Why? Simple, we reduce the pressure of *now* and understand we've got a mission that's designed to span decades, and hopefully, our lives. This doesn't mean we're complacent; it means we're able to sacrifice short-term benefits for long ones.

Remember, playing the long game doesn't necessarily mean it's going to take a long time. Rather, it's a mindset to help keep your eye on your bold vision and see obstacles as on the way, not *in* the way.

Leap Tip: Make Decisions About Who You're Becoming

The amateur makes decisions based on who he or she is today, and lets his or her circumstances bring them down. This is a surefire way to play and stay small, or at best achieve incremental growth.

Instead, every time you make a decision, do it by asking the following question: what would the person who has accomplished my vision decide?

Risk Pillar 3: Be in the Right Environments

If you've ever declared your bold vision to a family member, sibling, or co-worker, and they shot you down, you know how it feels. You put yourself on the line, and all they could come back to you with is:

"That won't work."
"That's not realistic—you need to go back to school."
"I wouldn't buy that … it's been done."

Quickly, your inspiration and drive start to fade, and you take this feedback at face value. This is the danger of being in an environment where risk taking is seen as bad, and the safe path should be your path.

Environment matters much more than we think, especially in regard to bold decisions and life changing moments. Later on, we'll explore the power of declaring your leap, but only to the *right* people.

By placing yourself in the right environment, you'll have the backbone of support required to ensure your success. Don't buy the hype, there is no such thing as self-made. Along your path, you'll find countless mentors, peers, and those who are likeminded helping you every step of the way. You'll meet the tribe designed to support your boldest aspirations. (We'll explore this deeper in Chapter 16, too.)

In other words, don't roll solo. Doing so has a shelf life, and you're unlikely to persist when adversity strikes if you're in the wrong environment. We all need this ecosystem to thrive, and it's your responsibility to insert yourself into those environments to ensure your success.

Flip the Script and Change the Rules

Now that we've examined how our perception of risk keeps us *stuck* and unfulfilled, it's time to flip the script, change the results and use risk in our favor.

Because here's the truth:

Staying at the soul-sucking job that is slowly destroying all of your enthusiasm and energy for life *is risky.*
Spending more time procrastinating on your dreams under the veil of doing more research and waiting for the right time *is risky.*
Rationalizing why you shouldn't ask him or her out the moment you feel you have to and succumbing to excuses *is risky.*
Living in a place that robs you of your creative genius and thrill for adventure is *risky.*

Right now, I want you to take a moment and identify one place where playing it safe is risky.

Now that you've done that, you're now armed with a new perspective designed to give you the clarity needed to use risk as your competitive advantage. There's no more waiting, hoping, praying, or wishing. You're about to discover what it feels like the moment you choose yourself in a world telling us we should choose anyone except ourselves.

The Greatest Risk of All

Giordano Bruno took the biggest risk one can take—trading his life for his conviction in what he believed in.

His mouth fitted with an iron gag and stripped naked, Bruno was led to Campo de Fiora in Rome on a brisk February morning. Unable to speak, he was tied to a stake. As they lit the flames that would end his life, Bruno looked up one last time at the wonders that drove him: the stars and the unknown Universe. For a moment, everything felt right.

Today, Campo de Fiora is a buzzing tourist hotspot in the middle of Rome. Surrounded by cafes, flower shops, and tourists sipping on local wine; the energy is palpable. Students, locals, and tourists mixed together, with a buzz in the air. In the middle of it all, sits a massive statue of Giordano Bruno.

Hundreds of years later, Bruno is seen as a beacon of free thinking, self-reliance, and courage. Although he wasn't able to live to see a day where his ideas and beliefs were widely accepted, Bruno's spirit and driving force created an undeniable legacy spawning centuries.

Now, you may be saying: there's no way I'm risking my life for the leap. I get it, and what you don't realize is you're *already* risking your life by not taking the leap.

And so, the greatest risk you and I can ever take is simple: not taking it. Now that we know the heavy price you're paying, it's time to pack your bags, get your essentials in order, and prepare for the journey ahead.

We've got no time to waste.

Chapter 4 Key Takeaways

- **Redefine risk or else.** We've been taught the safe path is less risky, but is it really? The greatest risk is not taking one and watching life pass us by. Redefine risk and use it as leverage for new opportunities.

- **Opportunity cost is real.** When we say yes to something, we automatically say no to another alternative. What if that alternative was a life you couldn't wait to wake up for? What are you automatically saying no to when looking at your life as it stands today?

- **Risk is influenced by environment.** The people, places, and mindsets we surround ourselves with will determine our ability to make bold decisions. Examine your environments to ensure you're in the right places.

CHAPTER 4 LEAP POWER STEP

Where in your life are you currently living in the illusion of safety and yet taking a massive risk? Flip the script and redefine why your circumstance is the riskiest place for you to stay in

_____

_____

_____

_____

Notes

1. http://discovermagazine.com/2008/sep/06-burned-at-the-stake-for-believing-in-science.

2. https://www.huffingtonpost.com/2014/09/04/the-alchemist-paulo-coelho-oprah_n_5762092.html.

PART

I

Turning Point: Letting Go

W e've gone deep on what's been holding you back and the cost of putting off your leap. We've identified the painful reality of regret, and how to redefine risk to serve your dreams. As we transition out of Part I, it's time to let go.

What got you here won't get you to where you want to go. Without letting go, your chances of reverting back are high. The pull to the past is engulfed in complacency and turns insight into yet another fantasy.

There's a part of you that is ready to be let go of, so you can create the space and capacity for what's coming. And while this belief, mindset, behavior, excuse or way of seeing the world may be part of your identity, it won't be going forward.

Complete the following questionnaire before moving on to Part II.

Part I Turning Point: Letting Go

Out of everything we covered in Part I, what resonated the most?

_____

_____

_____

_____

_____

Why did this specific piece resonate with you? Dig deep.

_____

_____

_____

_____

_____

What are you committed to letting go of? Be specific. Identify a behavior, a mindset, a habit, or belief that keeps you stuck.

_____

_____

_____

_____

_____

PART

II

Before Your Journey

Never forget that life can only be nobly inspired and rightly lived if you take it bravely and gallantly, as a splendid adventure in which you are setting out into an unknown country, to face many a danger, to meet many a joy, to find many a comrade, to win and lose many a battle.

—*Annie Besant*

Chapter 5

Know Yourself

Step out into your local city, and grab a person walking by on the street. Ask them about their life philosophy, the principles they live by, and how they integrate them into life. You'll get some blank stares, odd looks, and, if you're in New York, you're bound to get a special treat. Sometimes that treat comes in the form of a middle finger.

Before you set out on the voyage of your leap, you're going to have to know yourself. No, this isn't the superficial ways you already identity yourself. I'm talking on a *deep* level; know who you are, what you stand for and what you believe in, otherwise, you won't be able to build anything sustainable.

Knowing yourself sounds simple, but this is a journey few tackle. Often, people wait for a crisis moment to know themselves, because their identity has been stripped down and there's nothing left. Whether due to a crippling divorce, a financial loss, the death of a loved one, or a health scare, these moments leave *no option* but to engage in the questioning of self.

But it doesn't have to be that way. Relying on a crisis to take the path of self-discovery is not a strategy. We can also choose to face ourselves head on. We can use our past as leverage toward making bigger and bolder decisions. Without this crucial piece, the demands and intensity of your leap are likely to take over and you may never make it back to shore.

Ignorance Isn't Bliss; It's Painful

They say ignorance is bliss, but in the case of knowing yourself, it's painful. The cost of not knowing ourselves in life is rampant and leads to dire consequences. Without a foundation, we can feel lost. It's common to feel like we're going nowhere fast. Worse, even if we do become *successful*, we feel empty. Without introspection and self-discovery, it's impossible to feel deeply fulfilled and connected with ourselves. But this introspection is rare.

It's not that we don't have a longing for who we are, we simply distract ourselves from taking the inward journey. It's much easier to turn on YouTube or the latest Netflix show than sitting in silence and thinking about your life.

However tempting, the path of distraction, sedation, and avoidance leads to chaos and uncertainty. Consider knowing who you are to be the lighthouse on your journey.

Although they're rarely used these days, lighthouses sit at the most visible part of land near water, rooted to the ground. When visibility is high, they can be seen from up to 50 miles away. The light provides a trusted compass. During times of chaos and intense storms, lighthouses are designed to help those at sea come back to safe harbor.

This is knowing who you are. Having a backbone, a place you can lean on when the waves are increasing in intensity and the storm is right around the corner. In this chapter, we're going to explore who you are and how to integrate this wisdom into your leap.

A word of caution: many people like to skip this step. This part isn't sexy. It won't sell out arenas. And yet, those who skip it are the ones who most need it.

Otherwise, you may as well be taking your leap without a parachute on the way down.

Step 1: Cultivate Your Life Philosophy

A life philosophy isn't some esoteric, pie-in-the-sky statement you found at the Hallmark store scrambling for a birthday card last week. It's not something that sounds great on paper, it's a living, breathing testament of who you are.

Don't take this lightly. You're already *living* your philosophy, so now we're simply going to spend time identifying it and defining it. This process alone will give you incredible clarity.

Dr. Michael Gervais has spent thousands of hours with elite performers as a renowned sports psychologist. He was the go-to guy when Felix Baumgartner was experiencing anxiety with the rigidness of the Red Bull spacesuit. Because he was used to flying with the freedom of a skydiving suit, Felix dialed up Gervais when he was on the verge of quitting.

When asked about the most important piece of all performance, he said that having a life philosophy comes *first* and is often the most important piece:

> It may be the fundamental force that shapes how you experience life. You just need to uncover it. Your philosophy is revealed by the choices you make and the actions you take.[1]
>
> **—Dr. Michael Gervais**

Start thinking about what your life philosophy could be—What's the first phrase or sentence that comes to mind? Your first intuitive hit contains the gold, and there's no right or wrong answer.

However, to do it right, your life philosophy will need the following four components:

1. **It must be concise.** Ideally, a life philosophy is less than 25 words. If you need more, you're not clear enough. Drill it down until it becomes short and to the point.

2. **It must move you emotionally.** Your philosophy has to move you. Even declaring it should raise your heart rate and shift your awareness ever so slightly. You need to feel it within.

3. **It must be (truly) yours.** We're conditioned to say things that society wants for us, or what our parents told us we should say. Not here. This must be yours, and you must take complete ownership.

4. **You must show proof of living it**. A life philosophy isn't some future aspiration or hope. It's not an affirmation. It's a statement of who you are—and what you embody. Break down the word *embody*, and you notice it's saying, "in body." In other words, it's within.

Like everything in life, your philosophy will evolve. This is part of the human experience of growth. However, your life philosophy is a place you can always come back to during the ebb and flow of life.

Here are some examples of life philosophies (some of these summarized by me):

- Steve Jobs, Apple: Creative expression through technology
- Martin Luther King: Civil rights and nonviolence
- Pete Carroll, Seattle Seahawks: Compete every day
- John F. Kennedy: Dare to dream big
- Barack Obama: Hope

Your Life Philosophy

_____

_____

Leap Tip: Intuition Always Wins

When crafting your life philosophy, go with your gut (or intuition). Don't write down what others want for you, or what sounds great on a Hallmark card.

What are *you* about? What do you want to *be* about? Don't wait. Write 10 possibilities right now. Go with the one that feels best.

Step 2: Identifying Your Core Principles (or Values)

If your life philosophy was the summary of who you are, your core principles require a deeper look. They are the pillars of what make up your philosophy and how you actually get there. If your philosophy is the end result of a delicious meal, then your core principles are the *ingredients* you used to make it.

These principles are what you believe in, and they permeate every part of your experience: your thoughts, your thought patterns, your worldview, and your behaviors. Principles can also be called *values* and are a crucial step in self-awareness, fulfillment, and performance. Here's why:

1. **They make decision-making easy.** If integrity is one of your core principles, you're unlikely to pick up and keep the wallet you pass on the street. You're more likely to pick it up and take steps to return it to its rightful owner. You won't choose to start a pyramid scheme or lie to your partner. You're automatically going to only allow people, environments, and other things in life to support those principles.

2. **You're living them, but you also aspire to them.** The beauty of your principles is you're living them, and there's proof. But they're also a daily aspiration. Each day, you and I wake up and we either reaffirm these principles with our behaviors or we don't. This is the key separator between feeling aligned in our lives and feeling disconnected.

3. **They become your identity.** Your principles become who you are and are part of your identity. You base everything around them, and they give you certainty in the face of stress, anxiety, or unexpected circumstances.

Often, it can be beneficial to work the principles first, and then the life philosophy becomes apparent. There's no right or wrong way to do it. Here's what's required for you to identify your core principles:

1. **Choose three to five principles.** Keep them short and choose only the ones that speak to you deeply. If done right, they all support one another.

2. **Show proof you're living them.** Much like our life philosophy, we must show proof we're living these principles. Does that mean you're perfect? No, it means no matter what happens, you're always aspiring to them. They become a driving force in your life.

3. **Refine them every quarter.** Four times a year, spend time refining and retooling your principles. They won't dramatically shift, but life experiences, breakthroughs, and growth will always have an impact on our principles.

4. **Ask the (right) people for feedback.** A great exercise is to ask five people who know you for open and honest feedback. To do this right, it's often best to ask those who are slightly on the outside of our inner circle. Why? No emotional bias.

Now, identify the core principles you're currently living, or aspire to be living.

Your Core Principles

_____

_____

_____

_____

Now that we've explored your life philosophy and principles, it's time to harness the key skills of emotional intelligence and resilience. This essential skill will be at the core of knowing yourself.

#NotesFromTheLeap

Taylor Stone
Owner, Inner Goddess Health

What's the boldest leap you've ever taken and why was this important to you?

I started waking up without inspiration and my intuition kept telling me I had bigger things waiting for me. Without knowing what "it" was, I did know I had to leave my current situation, or I wasn't going to be able to fulfill my purpose. My dreams began to be very morbid and I started seeing signs and synchronicities that were telling me that I had to leave. I took action and packed up what could fit in my 4Runner and moved across the country.

What did you feel as you made this leap, and what happened after?

I was actually very excited and felt a sense of freedom and relief. I somehow knew everything was going to work out for me, and I had to trust. Now, I feel more alive, I am happier than I have ever been on every level and I am extremely fulfilled. It helped me to inspire more women to listen to their intuition and that the life they crave to live isn't so far out of reach if they take the leap.

Looking back, what would you tell someone else in a similar circumstance knowing what you now know?

It doesn't have to make sense logically, but it will feel good in your soul. You will get excited thinking about it, and what could be. Your mind will play games with you, your family will think you're crazy, but you have to do it anyways.

Step 3: Developing Emotional Intelligence and Resilience

Frequently, I'll have clients come to me looking to reach the *next level* of their business. They're looking to experience a breakthrough. They always come in thinking it's a strategy or a tactic that's going to get them there.

And they're *always* wrong. Sure, strategies and tactics have a place, but I first start in an unexpected place: examining their emotions. This includes starting with a deep look at what's going on under the hood, as emotions become roadblocks to clarity and execution.

Emotions are a daily practice, yet few of us have any training on how to use them as leverage for growth. One of the biggest drivers of discontent is our inability to understand our own emotions. It's the source of existential crisis, endless conflict, and the killer of dreams, relationships, and forward momentum.

Worse off, a lack of understanding our emotions can lead to terrible decisions. It leads to unnecessary conflicts with others, and an unhealthy relationship with ourselves. Since none of us have been taught how to handle our emotions, we're simply "winging" it and doing our best to figure them out. Understanding our emotions can be broken down into three distinct pillars:

1. **Emotional intelligence** or developing an understanding of our emotions. This is how quickly we can identify what's *really* happening with our emotions. I like to think of this much like Wi-Fi, and the more that you and I can improve the speed and strength of our signal, the better off we are.

2. **Emotional maturity,** the ability to rise above the common triggers of daily emotions (impatience, anger, frustration) and see yourself and the world around you from a much deeper perspective. At the core of emotional maturity is bucking the natural instinct to blame others and instead taking responsibility.

3. **Emotional resilience,** being able to wrestle with uncomfortable emotions and our ability to bounce back to find peace and clarity. Think of the last time you experienced an uncomfortable emotion that led you down a bad path. Emotional resilience is the ability to not only understand the emotion but also to minimize the energetic impact it has on you.

The problem? We haven't been trained on any of these, and we can easily fall prey to highly charged emotional states. Those who developed these three emotional pillars have been shown to:

1. **Handle adversity swiftly.** Challenges in our day-to-day lives can come with a hefty dose of emotional intensity, and usually the *initial* problem isn't the problem.
2. **Feel more inner peace.** Our ability to handle life's emotions ultimately gives us a sense of inner peace. This quiet calmness is not only a physical and mental benefit, but it prevents us from making decisions we're bound to regret later. Instead, we're able to connect with ourselves and understand that the intensity of the moment will pass.
3. **Be less reactive.** It's been a long day at work. You didn't sleep great last night, and today you have too much on your plate. As the day passes, triggers start to appear—you get cut off on the road, the Starbucks line takes too long, and the client *still* hasn't paid the invoice. Sigh.

An email comes in right before you close your laptop for the day, and instantly, anger strikes. You're pissed off, and you quickly hit the reply tab and type a scathing email. You feel great doing this and you know you're right. They're wrong, and it's their fault. The next morning you wake up with regret. You hope the email was happening during your second REM cycle. You check the phone—damn, it's there. You read it and you're shocked you would send such a thing.

In this case, a high level of emotional fitness would still *feel* the trigger, albeit reduced. However, it's what happens next that separates those with low emotional resilience and intelligence that matters. That next behavior, the next choice is everything.

So how do you develop your emotional capacity to deal with all life has to offer? Here's a simple six-step process designed to get you there:

The Six-Step Process to Develop Your Emotional Skillset
1. What am I feeling right now? Release judgment and simply identify the feeling.
2. Why am I feeling this way? Connect the dots.
3. Is feeling this way getting me closer to what I want or further away?
4. If the answer is yes, you're getting closer, you're done. You understand the emotion and have identified it is serving you.
5. If the answer is no, release the emotion.
6. Based on your release, choose to experience a new emotion that serves what you want.

Step 4: Radical Self-Assessment

Throughout the journey of knowing yourself, developing a routine of radical self-assessment will be crucial. Often, we allow our clarity to get clouded by living in a world of false narratives and beliefs that don't allow us to see *exactly* where we are.

This is my issue with dance party, motivational Red Bull seminars. Although I believe getting in peak emotional states to achieve clarity is important, they often only focus on the vison and possibility for your life. With the EDM dance beat at full blast and the dopamine to match, the energy is palpable.

But something is missing. Because most people who experience this energy will feel high for a week or two, and then it'll fade. One reason is the lack of radical self-assessment, or what I call *taking inventory*. It's impossible for you to build a dream or a vision without first knowing where you are.

Often, we're afraid to look at where we are, so instead we look at where we may be able to go. That feels better than:

- Reflecting on the career that's eating you alive and getting honest about how much your current path *isn't for you*.
- Looking in the mirror, both literally and figuratively to assess what you see reflected back to you in regard to physical performance, health, and vitality.
- Avoiding printing out your bank statements and spending time with your income numbers, because they're *not* pretty.
- Asking your life partner for real, honest feedback on how we're showing up because we'd rather live in assumptions.

So, how do you go about radical self-assessment? Simple: get honest about your current circumstances. Take a moment right now to reflect on your life, and ask yourself:

Do you have a sense of purpose and fulfillment with your work?
Do you have a connection to your body with health and vitality?
Do you have confidence you're on the right track with your life?
Do you have a powerful connection to your closest relationships?

Without excuses, simply answer these questions. If the answers are *no*—you're practicing radical self-assessment. This, then, becomes a daily practice during which you take a moment to cut off the noise and check in.

Leap Tip: Release the Emotion

None of us were trained to understand our emotions. Often, these lead to nonproductive activities and sometimes destructive ones.

Next time you feel *charged*, write down exactly what you're feeling. This is not a time to play nice: let her rip. This practice helps you identify what you're feeling and release it in a healthy way.

Expression is always a source of healing and ultimately—clarity.

Step 5: Examining and Reframing Your Stories

Stories are simply beliefs in action. These narratives become a guiding force to propel us through our experiences and end up shaping the quality of our lives.

Unexamined, stories can be crippling and push us farther away from what we *really* want, keeping us stuck for years on end. But they can also be used to inspire, empower, and create radical shifts you once thought were unavailable to you.

Our stories range from the all-encompassing, such as "I'm not good enough" to more specific, say, in the context of business "Everyone is out to get me" or "No one will outwork me" or "It's hard for me to communicate."

This is the inner dialogue we're constantly repeating and reaffirming hundreds, if not thousands, of times a day. So, why are stories so powerful?

1. **They determine the way we see the world.** The narrative we create will determine our perception. They're our beliefs being played out in real time, scene by scene.
2. **We play out the characters role within our stories**. Every narrative has characters, and the main one is the person going through your life: you. You're going to follow the script, whether you like it or not.
3. **They're the precursor to action or inaction.** Your stories either become a catalyst for action and growth or inaction and stagnation.
4. **They're deeply tied to our emotional state.** Earlier, we examined the power of emotional intelligence and resilience. Stories become a way to become beholden to our emotions or break free from them.

The great news is stories can also be transformed at any moment. They can be used as leverage to push you to grow and get you to your dreams faster. Part of knowing yourself is being able to examine the narratives you're currently walking around with, and asking a simple question:

Will this story or narrative serve the person I'm becoming and the vision of the leap I've created?

If the answer is no, here's your opportunity to create a new story. If the answer is yes, it's your chance to double or triple down and go *all in*. If this seems like a lot of work, don't fret.

I'll provide you some frameworks to examine your stories, simplify the process, and choose the stories you're committed to operating with throughout your leap, starting now.

For example, here are some of mine and how they impact my behaviors:

- *There is nothing I can't create when I pour my mind, body, and spirit into it.* This allows me to believe in what I'm doing on a deep level, and always find the "win" in any situation.
- *The only approval I require is the approval of the man looking back at me in the mirror.* This allows me to practice self-reliance and reminds me to not live based on other's approval or expectations of me.
- *I step into the unknown with faith, trust, and clarity.* This allows me to reframe the fear of the unknown, instead using it to my advantage to know it's what I *must* do.

What are the stories you're going to choose for your leap? Identify at least three right now (even if they're not currently true, but you're committed to making them true.)

Identifying Your New Stories

1. _____

2. _____

3. _____

Your Leap Is the Direct Path to Know Yourself

Change is *hard*. Despite the endless seminars on how you can make it big in real estate in three months and move to Cancun to sip margaritas for the rest of your life, human behavior is complex. It's messy, and there's no linear path, no matter what the personal development seminars are telling you.

Change that endures is even *harder.* Sure, it's easy to go low-carb or meditate for 30 days, but are you willing to completely shift your lifestyle for the rest of your life? For most, the answer is no, at least not long term.

Knowing yourself becomes a crucial ingredient for your leap. Although your leap will be the most invigorating thing you'll do, it's going to rock your identity. Any time we make big changes in life, we shift who we believe ourselves to be and it's a vulnerable place.

If you add the external stress and chaos of life to that equation and don't have a solid backbone, it can be a recipe for disaster. When you do the foundational work, and combine it with the leap of your life, you'll build a trust with yourself that nothing else on the planet can match.

By completing the Identify Your New Stories exercise, you've done a lot of the heavy lifting. And yet, you may still feel overwhelmed. That's precisely why it's time to release the noise, and get you clear.

Chapter 5 Key Takeaways

- **Knowing yourself provides a stable foundation.** Spend time doing the inner work of cultivating a philosophy, identifying your core principles, and taking inventory of where you are today. This is the best place to build from.

- **Emotional intelligence and resilience are skills.** Navigating your emotions is a skill, and one that pays off with clarity and inner peace. Ensure this is a daily practice.

- **Stories are belief-driven narratives.** Our stories shape our behaviors and can be placed in one of two categories: serving you or not serving you. Identify yours, and create new ones that *serve* your leap.

CHAPTER 5 POWER ACTIONS

Complete all of the work in this section before moving on. Don't overthink it but be intentional. Understand if you put pen to paper, you're in the 5% of people who take the time to do the much-needed inner work.

Notes

1. https://www.thriveglobal.com/stories/23421-living-in-alignment-with-your-personal-philosophy.

Chapter 6

Release the Noise

By all accounts, Karan Baraj seems like your typical Fortune 500 executive. He lives in Manhattan, has a toddler, buys $14 green juice and has worked hard to climb the ranks of the corporate ladder. Along the way he's experienced success, including being named "top 40 under 40" executives in marketing by *Ad Age*.

Pretty standard, right? It may seem that way, but every four years Karan rips his life wide open and takes his family with him on a trip with no plan, purpose, or outcome. He spends time in ashrams across the Himalayas, waking up early to scrub the monastery, and spends hours in meditation. He travels on a whim, writes novels, and stops setting personal goals. He leaves his corporate gig behind with little to no communication along the way.

After a year, he comes back and re-enters society for another four years—until the cycle repeats itself. Calling this the 4–1–4 model, Karan expands during our interview:

> In the year that I take off I'm very consciously goal-less. I completely strip myself of the entire idea of becoming. I make both physical and emotional decisions in line with

that. For instance, in the last sabbatical, my wife and I had a very clear intention that we didn't want to plan a single day at all. We wanted to only make decisions that were completely intuitive and natural that came from within.[1]

Karan is a trailblazer; his novels have been optioned for movies, and he's one of India's bestselling authors of all time. Clearly, his unconventional approach is paying off. For most in the corporate world (or even entrepreneurs), this setup would seem like an utter pipe dream. Logistics aside, unplugging from the world means facing our fears head on: fears of missing out, falling behind, or tuning out from society. Who are we when we're not participating in the marathon of modern culture?

Yet, there is something special to it. We all long for this ability to disconnect from the revolving treadmill that becomes our lives at some point. Karan's sabbatical lifestyle is an example of the power of releasing the noise, an essential component you'll need before, during, and after your leap.

Because deep down, **you already know what to do.**

You Already Know What to Do

"Uh, I don't know … this is *why* I hired you," he told me, visibly frustrated. I held the silence for a moment, and the tension was palpable.

"You already know what to do. You know your purpose, you've simply been unwilling to cut the noise and tap into it. You are letting fear own you. You are letting your head win."

This continued for two-and-a-half hours, until finally, after deep conversations and practices designed to reveal layers, he let it out. He already knew what he had to do yet was afraid.

He was afraid of expressing it, first to himself and then to me. Here was an entrepreneur with a big family. He had built a business in an industry his family hated, and they were coming clean for the first time on what they *really* wanted to do. But he knew this for a long time, and it was eating at him. Even though he claimed he needed clarity, he already knew what to do.

And so do you.

You Don't Discover Anything...You Allow It

There isn't a week that goes by when I'm not asked a variation of how-I-find-my- purpose-or-passion style questions. I get these questions from people who hire me and from people I've never met on social media, and the answer is always the same:

You're asking the *wrong* question. Your purpose, and your leap isn't something you go out and get, it's something you allow. **It's already within you, within all of us.** You've simply blocked the signal, because there's way too much noise in your life getting in the way.

Part of this can be strategic, of course. If our purpose and leap are something we have to go out and find, we can put off doing the work. The entire idea of finding something outside of ourselves comes with a degree of friction. It leaves us off the hook from living boldly.

Ask my fiancée what a pleasure I am to deal with when I can't find my car keys or wallet, and it's the same exact energy as the pressure of finding one's purpose: stressed, anxious, and scattered. In this state, creation is impossible.

And yet, the way I define purpose has nothing to do with friction and effort. It's what you *can't* do. And if not doing it eats away at you, then there's an alignment that comes with this type of energy.

The same goes for the *leap* you must take. It's in there, even if you claim you have no idea what to do.

Less Is More

The leap of your life is never about adding more things on an overloaded foundation. It isn't about spending years trying to figure out an answer. It's not about searching for clarity on an endless loop that never bears the fruit you're looking for. It's not about trying to figure yourself out for the next decade.

It's about *releasing* the noise. When I say this, I mean removing the obstacles you've put in the way, which are now keeping you stuck. They keep you frustrated and playing small, and in some instances, they are a brilliant strategy to not have to show up with courage.

The truth is you're already good enough. You are already worthy. You are capable.

It's time to make this a mechanism of the past, through a system I've used on thousands of people to reduce the obstacles in the way and allow for clarity to arrive. Armed with this clarity, your leap will never be the same.

Without it, you may as well never get started.

The Closet Principle

When I moved from New York to Arizona, I realized how mind-blowing walk-in closets are. Back East, closet space came at a premium, and you could forget about walking in anywhere, unless you had hit the big time. When I first came out West, I didn't know what to do with all that space.

As time went on, I had filled the closet with new clothes, outfits, luggage, and more. There was so much space, I chose to double its use as a meditation room. One day, I walked in and realized there was nowhere to go anymore; all the space had been taken up.

Interesting, I thought. I started to look around, and noticed I'd accumulated tons of stuff. New shirts, outfits, random clothing or stuff people had sent me. And that's when I realized: I'm only using 20% of things in here, and I'm wearing those 80% of the time.

Our lives parallel our closets: we have a certain amount of space, time, and energy available to us. We fill it up, and then realize most of the stuff we've filled our lives with we don't need. I started to call this

The Closet Principle (creative, right?), and I now use this example with my clients all the time.

The Closet Principle, of course, is the prominent 80/20 rule in action. The 80/20 rule is as universal as gravity, and comes up time and time again:

You wear 20% of your clothing 80% of the time.
You eat 20% of the same foods 80% of the time.
You hang out with 20% of people 80% of the time.

The list goes on and on, and while primarily introduced as an economic principle by an Italian economist named Vilfredo Pareto,[2] we can use this to streamline our lives and focus on what really matters, including:

The 20% of people who make you the happiest.
The 20% of your time that brings you fulfillment.
The 20% of powerful conversations that create connection.

Otherwise, we cannot only get lost in the *chaos* of overload, we can dangerously start putting our attention on what doesn't matter. In the case of the closet, even though I wear 20% of the same shirts, shoes, socks, and pants 80% of the time, I still have to make that decision every single day.

And those decisions add up day after day, leaving you and me with *less* clarity for the rest of our lives, and leading to more anxiety, procrastination, and a lack of results. It's no wonder we feel disconnected with ourselves.

Releasing the noise is about creating bandwidth for your life not only to focus on what *really* matters but also deleting what doesn't. It's about tuning into your signal, leveling up your environment, and ensuring your leap is a huge success.

Leap Tip: 80/20 Everything

The 80/20 rule can and will transform your life. Whether it's the 20% of customers that bring in 80% of the revenue, 20% of a city's streets with 80% of the traffic, it's everywhere.

Identify what you can delete from your life, to create space, clarity, and peace. Choose at least 20 things you can discard right now and don't look back.

Step 1: Take Inventory

The first step toward releasing the noise is knowing *what* the noise is. Taking inventory, then, becomes a powerful practice to identify what's taking up space in your life, and making an honest assessment about its place. From there, it's time to choose to keep it in your life or discard it.

This is best done by asking a question, and the one I use is simply: **Does this pull me closer to my leap's vision, or push me farther away?** (Don't worry if you don't have this ready yet, we'll cover it during the next two chapters.) The key here is to ensure radical honesty.

Much like our closets, we all have the article of clothing we don't wear but brings us nostalgia. And yet, this is precisely what we want to avoid; in the process of your leap, you must forget about who you've been and instead focus on who you're becoming. This is no time to sugarcoat why your high school buddy turned deadbeat should be someone you text every single day even though you haven't seen each other in two decades.

So, what precisely are you taking inventory of?

- **Beliefs.** We're going to spend an entire section on this later, but there are beliefs you can consciously identify right now that are holding you back and will continue to do so.
- **People.** The fact is, there's someone taking space in your life *today* that shouldn't be there. I know it and you know it. This isn't a selfish deal, because you're not serving them (or yourself) by holding on.

- **Environments.** We'll examine this in a moment, but our environments are the easiest *leverage* points to achieve change. Leverage in this context simply means the low hanging fruit that produces the largest result with the *least* amount of effort.
- **Noise.** Last, it's time to take inventory of the *noise* of your life. When I say noise, it's your smartphone, the media you consume, all of the communication, stimuli, and more.

These are the core categories you're going to take inventory of now to identify if they are moving you closer or farther away from your vision. For this step, there's no sense in judging or getting mixed up in emotional reasons that you need something. Using the preceding categories and having the courage to evaluate with honesty is more than enough.

Now that we've taken inventory, it's time to create some much-needed *space*.

Step 2: Delete, Delete, Delete

In Japan, crowded cities and an overloaded population means space is scarce and comes at a premium. After generations of limited personal space, a rush hour that lasts all day, and extremely rigid rules on common activities such as collecting trash, it has become commonplace to maximize every square inch.

Literally.

Often, even those who are well off don't have the luxury of having space for say an overnight guest. Known to be respectful and courteous, the Japanese culture is extremely efficient.

The truth is: they have *no other* option. In 2014, a concept from the tight spaces of Japanese culture came to the United States and took it by storm. Marie Kondo's *The Life-Changing Magic of Tidying Up*[3] stormed the country and has now sold over five million copies.

The premise is simple: **let go of anything you don't love**. Particularly, if it doesn't bring you joy, it's time to move on.

This is exactly what we're looking to do now that we've taken inventory — it's time to create space in your life by deleting what doesn't serve you anymore. Often, this act alone provides immense clarity, calm, and peace. Some examples include:

- Donating the 80% of clothing you don't use
- Decluttering your office and work space
- Getting rid of digital noise and apps
- Unfriending negative people on social media
- Organizing the messy garage full of clutter
- Deleting old text message threads
- Letting go of social commitments
- Deleting all notifications on your phone

Beyond the physical benefits, the deletion of *stuff* that we've accumulated allows for something new to come in. And that *new* thing is what will support your leap in ways you could have never imagined. Kondo expands on the power of discarding:

> The place we live should be for the person we are becoming now — not for the person we have been in the past.[4]

Deleting won't be easy. You've become used to certain beliefs, people, environments, and noise that feel great to you. Even if you understand they're not serving you, it can be difficult to let go. But let go you must, and allow the space for something much greater and empowering to take its place.

Step 3: Examine Your Environment

BJ Fogg, PhD, has been studying human behavioral change at Stanford University for two decades and running the Persuasive Tech Lab. After his decades of research on what *truly* creates change, he came to the following conclusion: "There's just one way to radically change your behavior: radically change your environment."[5] Earlier, I mentioned the power of leverage, or identifying the simplest changes that breed the *biggest* results. Environment, if used wisely, becomes the easiest path to transformation, but it can also be an anchor holding us back to the past.

Here's why. Our minds are designed for *extreme* efficiency. Part of this mechanism is using environmental cues to execute behaviors. When you walk into your bathroom in the morning, you're hard wired to pick up the toothbrush the same way you did yesterday, start brushing your teeth, and put it back. All *without* thinking.

Although that's a benefit you and I take for granted, there's one drawback: because we're wired for efficiency and recognizing patterns to dictate behavior, **environmental cues can easily hold us back as much as they can push as forward.**

One of the most controversial blog posts I've done to date has been *Why (Real) Entrepreneurs Don't Work From Home.*[6] I argued that attempting to do creative and focused work in the same environment where we, say, play with our kids, watch television, or connect with a partner isn't conducive to maximizing our output. As predicted, those who work from home ridiculed me, sending me their accolades on *why* working from home was key to their success.

Duke University psychologist and Professor of Neuroscience Wendy Wood studies effective behavioral change. She says: "Many of our repeated behaviors are cued by everyday environments, even though people think they're making choices all the time."[7] In other words, **environment matters much more than we're led to believe.** And if we do experience success, who's to say it wasn't *in spite* of our environment? We often believe that if we push through and want something bad enough, we'll overcome our environment.

The problem with this is motivation ebbs and flows based on our emotional states. Although we may be able to push through at times, friction adds up and never becomes a sustainable framework for enduring success, especially when we're exhausted after a long day and our willpower is running on empty.

To make your leap a rousing success, it's time to shift your environment. Make no mistake, an unexamined environment that doesn't support your leap may be the domino that holds you back. Don't take this lightly, and remember everything is fair game, including:

- **Is your physical environment supporting your leap?** Examine all your living environments from the top down, where you live physically—that is, your state, city and town—and then your micro-environments of your home, apartment, bedrooms, and so on.
- **Is your work environment supporting your leap?** Whether you're working for yourself as an entrepreneur, head to an office every day, or are still a student, examine your work environments. Are they conducive to your discipline, focus, and creative growth?
- **Is your play and relax environment supporting your leap?** Think of the places you have fun, let go, and use to relax. The places where you recharge and take life less seriously. Are they serving you long term, or are they leaving you worse off?
- **Is your health and wellness environment supporting your leap?** Examine where you train yourself physically—a home gym, a membership, hiking, and so on. Do these create powerful results and consistency for you?
- **Is your study and learning environment supporting your leap?** Look at all the places you learn—whether that's how and where you watch content, seminars, do reading, and more. Are they putting you in the *best* place to not only create insights, but also create results?
- **Is your spiritual environment supporting your leap?** Finally, look at the places where you connect with yourself spiritually. This could be a traditional religious practice, or a set of spiritual tools and rituals you use.

If the answer is no, it's time to shift. Your shift may be leaving your at-home office to find creativity in a co-working space. It could be moving to a new place. It may look like shifting your home environment to be more conducive with your goals. By doing so, you'll release the energetic toll of willpower and experience less decision fatigue. You'll have an abundance of mental and emotional energy to use on the important things, including your leap.

Step 4: Tune into the Signal

You've done the hard work that most aren't willing to do by releasing the noise. Remember, the noise is tempting. It's sexy, it's loud, and it can be a whole lotta fun. It's instant gratification, and we're being conditioned and hardwired to be engulfed in it every single day.

But now you've gone through the process of releasing the noise—a courageous endeavor most say they want, but don't follow through on. Now it's time to start tuning into the signal, *your* unique signal. When I say signal, I simply mean the inner wisdom we all have.

Within this place, you'll find the answers to life's deepest questions. You'll encounter the vision that brings you to your knees. Tuning into your signal is a practice and must be treated as such. The theme of treating it as a practice allows you to have a long-term mindset. Furthermore, practicing is focused, intentional work with the end result of improving a specific *skill*.

We'll expand on that later, but first let's identify some of the easiest and most accessible practices you can start using today to tune into your signal:

- **Nature.** One of the fastest paths to access your signal, spending time in nature can bring you the answers to your most pressing questions and provide invaluable insights.
- **Walking.** Walking, often called a *standing meditation* is a brilliant way to achieve a new perspective and connect to yourself on a deeper level.
- **Meditation.** What most people miss out on with meditation is trying to do it *right*. There is no right or wrong, there simply is. With meditation, you're not only accessing your signal, but working on the skill of focused concentration *and* emotional intelligence.
- **Float tanks.** Floating, or sensory deprivation, is meditation on steroids. This is one of my favorite ways to tune in, and the physical sensation of zero gravity will take you to incredible places.
- **Deep texts.** Reading a deep text designed to open your mind leads to powerful inner reflection. In this place, you're in tune with yourself and more likely to create time to *think* and press the pause button on life.

- **Thinking time**. Last, spending idle time *without* a specific agenda, simply thinking about life, your place in it, and whatever may come to mind. This is rare, yet all the greatest minds who changed the course of our world spent a significant amount of time thinking.

Leap Tip: Create Space (Start with One)

Pick one practice to start tuning in and reconnecting with the signal. For the next 30 days, you're going to do it every single day. Keep it simple and remember: the time you spend in this practice will pay off in massive ways.

This is far from a comprehensive list, but the underlying result is the same: helping you release the noise and find a state of inner peace.

Tuning Out to Tune Back In

Although noise can be addicting, once released, you'll experience a sense of calm and peace. You'll also start to notice new insights on a daily basis, leading you to be proactive, not reactive. In a world where we're always waiting for someone or something else to give us permission, or insight, you'll begin to trust yourself with more depth.

Trust becomes your inner guidance system before, during, and after your leap. It'll allow you to make decisions from a place of abundance, not scarcity. It'll get you tuned in and connected with yourself, leading to a deeper connection with others.

Some of the most powerful shifts and breakthroughs have come, not when I was standing in my office with a whiteboard, but in a deep meditation or while pushing myself up a mountain during a hike. With the sweat pouring off my face and the brisk Arizona sun making its mark for the first time in the morning, I get a *hit*.

And that hit is a powerful download of clarity and perspective that changes *everything*. And I'm here to tell you: you can do the same, if you're willing to harness the power coming from your own signal.

Because what you have inside of you once we've peeled back all the layers of fear, insecurity, doubt and your past is quite simply, pure gold. Now that you've released the noise, created space, and tuned into the signal, it's time to light your life on fire through purpose and passion.

Chapter 6 Key Takeaways

- **Release the noise to achieve clarity.** We often know what to do, yet our lives are too full of noise. To get clear, we must create space and let go of what's in the way.
- **80/20 everything.** We spend most of our time and energy on things that don't move the needle, and only 20% on the most essential. Creating a practice to cut out the remaining 80% will shift your game.
- **The power of deletion.** We are overworked, overcommitted and overstimulated. It's time to clear your plate and focus on deletion and creating space in your life.

CHAPTER 6 LEAP POWER STEP

It's time to delete. Make a list of 10 things you're choosing to let go of or eradicate from your environment. Think: physical environment, home, digital, work, office, social commitments, etc. **I am choosing to delete the following, in order to create more space:**

1. _____
2. _____
3. _____
4. _____
5. _____
6. _____
7. _____
8. _____
9. _____
10. _____

Notes

1. Resist Average Academy. Ep. 47. https://itunes.apple.com/us/podcast/resist
   -average-academy-knowledge-inspiration-action/id1073462154?mt=2.
2. https://www.amazon.com/80-20-Principle-Secret-Achieving
   /dp/0385491743.
3. https://www.amazon.com/Life-Changing-Magic-Tidying-Decluttering
   -Organizing/dp/1607747308.
4. https://www.dmaorganizing.com/2015/12/15/5-best-quotes-from-the-life
   -changing-magic-of-tidying-up/.
5. https://www.psychologytoday.com/us/blog/habits-not-hacks/201408/want
   -change-your-habits-change-your-environment.
6. https://resistaverageacademy.com/why-real-entrepreneurs-dont-work-from
   -home.
7. https://today.duke.edu/2007/12/habit.html.

Chapter 7

Light Your Life on Fire

When was the last time you *lost* yourself? Time dissolved, and you tapped into an energy more powerful than the daily Starbucks caffeine hit. You felt in the zone and connected. You not only didn't want it to end, it seemed impossible to stop. If it's been ages, that's okay, too. What matters is you have it, and it never goes away. Even if it's been years or you felt it yesterday, this energy is fundamental for your leap.

Lighting your life on fire applies to every leap in your life; it's rooted in living your purpose and allowing your passions to shine. When this happens, you're likely to enter a *flow* state, a blissful state of optimized performance. But simply beyond achieving double the results in half the time, these states are deeply fulfilling, both in business and life.

But before you're able to harness the true power of these states, you're going to have to get clear on your purpose, passion, interests, and skills (see Figure 7.1). Using these ingredients, you'll be able to move forward powerfully with your leap like never before.

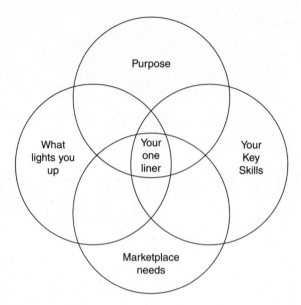

Figure 7.1   Purpose, passion, skills, and marketplace needs come together to create your one-liner.

Step 1: Create Clarity Around Your Purpose

We sat there in a poorly lit, and way-too-cold Houston conference room and were told we had to identify our life purpose. We had exactly 90 minutes. The timer started.

Shit, I thought. I felt tremendous pressure wash over me. I wrote, rewrote, and erased several sentences. I didn't know what I was doing, and I felt lost. Nothing I wrote stuck, and it all seemed like what I *should* be writing. I didn't know if I was writing my life purpose or entering a submission for Hallmark. When I looked around the room, I exhaled. It seemed everyone was having the same experience.

Here's why: if you and I are supposed to identify our life purpose, we better get it right. And that level of pressure is exactly the *wrong* way to think about it.

Purpose and Pressure Don't Mix

There's never been a time with such an abundance of energy dedicated toward discussing purpose, work, and meaning. This discussion has not only gone mainstream, it's accepted everywhere. And while that's awesome, the idea of clarifying a life purpose can seem daunting at best—and downright unbearable at worst.

It's time to shift our definition of purpose to what it really is: an *evolution*. Purpose, contrary to conventional wisdom, is never a destination. It will shift, develop, change, and transform countless times. This is the essence of an evolution. Depending on where you are in your life, it will look and feel differently. Knowing this, in turn, allows you to release the pressure and live your purpose *now*.

Purpose is based on who you are today, your current perspective, and where you're headed. You may be thinking: How can I live my purpose today, if I'm spending time in a career or situation that I know *isn't* right? This sounds cool, but I still can't stand my boss.

Here's how: **the core essence of your purpose is one thing, and the way you deliver this purpose to yourself, to those around you, and to the marketplace is what I call the *vehicle of delivery*.**

If you've decided the essence of your purpose is to *teach*, then the vehicle of delivery to get there can take different forms. Most importantly, you can activate your purpose muscle today, and not do what 99% of people do: wait and complain about how it's not working out for them. Whether you're a salesman, a grocery store clerk, mother, or full-fledged entrepreneur, you can still fulfill the essence of your purpose by teaching every single day. This not only makes you feel more connected with your work, you're already putting in essential practice needed to improve your craft.

Win, win.

For me, my purpose is to teach and inspire and to create space where people achieve a breakthrough leading to a radical increase in quality of life. This is a bit more defined (can you tell I've done this more than once?)

and yet, I *could* be doing a host of things: doing what I do now through consulting, coaching, writing and podcasting, or I could be a seventh-grade math teacher.

Okay, let me change that. I'm terrible at math and squeaked by every year with the most bottom-of-the-barrel C− you can find, but you get the point. I'd still be able to live and fulfill a *part* of my purpose, even if the vehicle of delivery wasn't perfect. The ultimate goal is for your essence and your vehicle to be in alignment. But waiting to work on your craft is never a good idea. Seth Godin, author of countless books including *Linchpin*, expands on this very same topic:

> Transferring your passion (and purpose) to your job is far easier than finding a job that happens to match your passion.

What he means is simple: waiting to live your purpose is a false premise: **if you haven't *practiced* your purpose, you won't magically wake up one day and live it full tilt.** Regardless of the vehicle, you haven't put in the required reps.

During the rest of this chapter, we're going to get you clear on a few essential ingredients for *any* leap while clarifying the essence of your purpose as it stands this moment.

Step 2: Identify What Lights You Up Inside

Right now, there are things you do that *light you* up inside. All this means is you lose yourself in them, no one has to remind you to do them and you love spending your most valuable and finite resources on them: your money/*time*.

The second key ingredient for your leap is to identify what lights you up, or what most people refer to as passion. Again, the common literature around this topic leaves most people wondering *how the hell* they're going to find their passion. The idea of having to go out and discover something when you're already overwhelmed means nothing happens.

And then you feel worse.

Often, I'll hear a variation of: "Tommy, I'm not sure what I'm passionate about." To that, I say *bullshit*. We all already have things we're passionate about and we don't need to hit the mountains of Peru and sit Indian style in a medicine wheel sipping on tea to figure them out.

So, how do we clearly identify our passions? How do we know something can be incorporated into a business and monetized, or remain a hobby? How can you strategically spend enough time in something to obtain the valuable knowing it's for you—or not for you? Why is the pursuit of mastery of a skill your competitive advantage in an Instagram famous world?

These are all great questions we're going to explore following a simple process designed to get you undeniably clear.

Identifying Your Passion(s)

It's time to identify what lights you up. They give you energy when you're tired. They move you when you don't feel great. They're what you think about and do when you've got free time. This is a passion. Don't judge what comes up, instead focus on how they make you *feel*.

It could be movies, stand-up comedy, learning, writing, cooking, gardening, training physically, hiking, nature, pets, personal development, finances, Feng shui, language—and the list goes on and on.

Take a moment to identify the common themes that come up time and time again that make you excited to be alive. These are your current passion(s) and there's no right or wrong. Now is not the time to focus on monetizing or any other pressure you've been told to put on them.

Identifying Your Interest(s)

Second, we're going to identify some of your core interests. These carry less energetic weight than passions, but they're still important. The difference? You haven't spent the same amount of time with your interests than you have your passion.

In any interest, it's worth spending enough time and energy on it to cross the threshold from complete novice to beginner. Otherwise, you truly don't know if it's simply an interest, a passion, or something you're ready to discard. Usually, this happens at about the 20-hour mark, according to Josh Kaufman who gave a TED talk on skill acquisition called *The First 20 Hours—How to Learn Anything.*[1]

For example, it's easy to get excited about playing the guitar. You get the right equipment, you start cranking YouTube tutorials feeling destined to become the next Eddie Van Halen. But at about the 20-hour mark, you realize something: this is hard, and that 16-year-old YouTuber player is *amazing*. It may take you 24 months to get anywhere near her level, and then you'd have to figure out singing. This is where you either choose to stick with it or move on.

There's value in distinguishing between your passion(s) and your interest(s). Some things deserve to stay as interests. You may love music: listening to it, going to concerts, and reading album reviews. But as much as you're interested in it (and sometimes feel flashes of passion for it), it's not at the level of passion today.

For the purpose of this exercise, you're going to make a list of your passions and interests as they stand today. If you can't figure out which one should go where, it's usually going to be an interest (for now).

Once we have your passions and interests, it's time to combine them with the third ingredient that makes you valuable in any marketplace: your skillset.

Step 3: Take Inventory of Your Key Skills

Although passion is sexy and will sell out motivational seminars, they mean little unless paired with skill acquisition. We're led to believe that if we're enthusiastic enough, people will automatically want to be involved with our work. Although this may be true at times, it's not a powerful foundation for long-term success.

These days, passion is normal. When I opened the doors to my original fitness facility, I believed I'd bring more energy and passion than anyone else. I was right. You could find me at the facility at 4:07 a.m. cranking music, high-fiving people and being *that* way, too—annoyingly positive guy who you can't stand up before I've had my morning brew.

(I'm still him, and my fiancée would agree.)

And yet, what I learned the hard way was passion *wasn't* enough. If you build it, they won't always come. I had to develop a set of skills to differentiate myself in the marketplace and become proficient at reaching the people I wanted to serve. I could be the best in the world, but if no one knew about me I'd always be struggling.

With this insight, I focused on the skill of copywriting, crafting an influential and persuasive message to connect with people. Make no mistake—handwriting 4,000-word sales letters to start one's day is *no fun*. But as time passed, I realized the combination of passion for one's work and skill acquisition is what makes us lethal in any marketplace. Often, this combo is undervalued.

In 2012, professor, academic, and writer, Cal Newport, published *So Good They Can't Ignore You*. Borrowing a line from comedian Steve Martin about where to place one's focus in one's craft, the book is an argument against fully following one's passion. Although I agree with most of the premise, I find the truth to be in the middle: passion *is* important but combining it with essential skills is the gamechanger.

So, what are your core skills? You may be an amazing listener and you're the one people lean on in crisis. You may be able to take complex financial jargon and make it digestible to someone like me. You may understand influence and its place in social media.

Identify your core skills and then place them into the following categories:

- **Beginner.** You've developed *some* skill, but recognize you are still in the beginner phase. (Usually 20–200 hours.)
- **Intermediate.** You've spent time refining a skill and have received feedback on your proficiency. You're above average in it. (Usually 200–1,000 hours.)

- **Professional.** You're at an elite level. Here is where people throw opportunities your way because of your level of skill. (Usually 1,000–10,000 hours.)
- **Mastery.** You're in rarified air and are considered world class. This is a rare spot and takes decades of focused work to accomplish. (Usually 10,000–30,000 hours.)

These categories can be subjective. But there's enough distinction among them to drop your skills into the appropriate category for now. Later in the chapter, you'll find out how to evaluate your current skills, and create a game plan in line with your purpose, passions, and your leap.

Step 4: Examine the Marketplace and Their Needs

There comes an elegant intersection between your core purpose— what lights you up and your current inventory of skills—where they're blended to provide value to others.

At the end of the day, all we can do to increase our value on the world is help others solve problems. Whether that problem is finding a place to crash, hailing a ride from a (hopefully trustworthy) stranger, getting unstuck in business, or finally losing the last 15 pounds, there's no problem too small or insignificant.

Using the following question, you're going to start to fill in the blanks by doing a marketplace brain dump. This is about letting your imagination run *wild* with options. Don't judge them, and don't put any pressure on why something may or may not work. No idea is off the table, because working through options will increase your creativity.

You do this by asking a simple question: Given everything I've just uncovered, **what problems are currently in the marketplace that I could provide solution(s) for?**

There are all types of people with all types of problems *you* could be the one helping them find a solution. To get the ideas flowing, you'll need to identify at least 20 solutions. Surely, you'll discard most, but there are going to be two or three from this list that connect with you.

They strike a chord for several reasons: you spot an opportunity, it feels right to you, and it blends all the things you already love *while* being connected to the purpose statement.

With this in hand, it's time to clarify it down into one concise statement to ensure you're clear and so are the people you're looking to serve.

Step 5: Construct Your One-Liner

What do you do?

"I, uh . . . I do real estate."

My client was playing small; he provided people with an experience unlike any other when purchasing a home. But here he was falling into a common trap: minimizing himself and missing countless opportunities.

When most people are faced with this question, they either play small or lack clarity. The truth is, **if you're lacking clarity, then the marketplace will, too.** Sometimes, we're unwilling to have clarity due to telling others *who we really are.* Often, we're afraid to declare what is most important to us for fear of not being good enough. As a writer, it can be daunting to declare I am one. Why? Because now I'm on the hook. I've put myself out there and declared to the world what I am, and I have to live it every single day.

One of the most powerful exercises I've done for my businesses and my clients comes from Donald Miller of Story Brand.[2] His exercise, called the *One-liner,* is what it sounds like: distilling what we *do* into a concise, clear, and compelling sentence or two.

Miller developed the one-liner from the Hollywood world, where a screenplay is approved or rejected based on a few sentences. If it was compelling enough, it'd make the next stage. What he realized was all effective one-liners were broken down into three distinct parts. These included:

The problem you're solving. This is where it all starts, and how you can connect with people immediately. Why? Because often, we're all in our own worlds, focusing on our problems and what we need solutions for. The moment you can declare what's going on in someone else's life as well as they can, you have connection.

For example:

"Travel is incredibly stressful."

"Learning guitar can take triple the time it should if you don't do it right."

"Moving cross-country can be the most chaotic experience of your life."

"Most entrepreneurs have no problem creating a bold vision; it's what happens after."

Simple, concise, and to the point, the problem is designed to *hook* the right person into learning more. Emphasis on the word right: if they have the problem you're declaring.

The process you use to solve the problem. Once the problem has been stated, it's time to transition into the unique process you use to create the solution to the problem. Using the preceding examples, we continue:

"Using our patented process and relationships with top airlines and airports…"

"Our system has been proven on thousands of frustrated guitar students all over the world…"

"Our done-for-you, nationwide service eliminates guesswork and helps you focus on what matters."

"Through comprehensive coaching, consulting, and content…"

The payoff, or solution. Last, we finish with the payoff, solution, and/or benefit the person is bound to experience by solving this problem. This is the resolution and the clear *after*. For our preceding examples, these are:

> *"Allowing you to skip the lines and arrive at your destination with peace of mind."*
>
> *"Give you all the tools you need to become a great guitar player in half the time."*
>
> *"You'll have the smoothest move of your life."*
>
> *"Helping you reverse engineer your success in half the time."*

Simple, right? I've been taught this exercise countless times and have performed it on my clients. This is a simple rundown, and if you want to learn more, make sure to visit Donald Miller's work in the Resources section.

No matter where you find yourself today, **clarity is a process, never a destination**. That means refining and re-imagining your one-liner must be done *at least* once a quarter as both you and your business grow and expand. Even if you're currently working for someone else, go through this process and come up with the one-liner you'd like to have.

This instantly creates a shift in your mind and compels you to make more powerful decisions and business leaps to make your one-liner real.

Mastery Creates Meaning

Meaning is what we all want to feel in our lives and work. We want to feel we're valued and making someone else's life better. Part of mastery, as introduced earlier, is the acquisition of skills to help you become valuable. Through the process of identifying, practicing, refining, and integrating these skills, you improve. In a noisy digital world where most seek shallow, right-on-time skills, you separate yourself from the pack and start to fall in love with your craft.

Part of this equation is creating a skill focus and refinement plan for your success, which we'll tackle now.

Your Skill Game Plan

I'm throwing a ton at you, for good reason: this is the gold that will ensure your leap is a success; it's a system to get you on a path of expertise and mastery others will willingly pay for. Let's take what we've discussed earlier and break it down in an actionable, practical path for you to start using today.

Step 1: Brain Dump

Your first step in the skill-acquisition process is to put pen to paper. Specifically, identify all the possible skills you could work on to enhance your purpose, passion, and business. Don't worry about their validity, write whatever comes to mind. Aim for at least 30.

Step 2: Categorize

Once you've completed your brain dump, it's time to categorize your skills in the different categories we identified earlier in the chapter. Don't overcomplicate this; it's pretty obvious where we find ourselves on our skill path. If you can't decide between intermediate and professional, you're an intermediate. Feel free to ask others for feedback, but don't get lost in doing so.

Step 3: Deletion

Next, you're going to step away for at least an hour and come back to your list. Now, you're going to delete up to 80% of your list and ensure what remains is the essential. Note: some of these are skills you want to pursue, but it's not the right time or season for it.

Step 4: Focus

Now, you're going to identify the two core skills you're going to strategically focus on during the next six months. Ensure these are only the highest level in value for your current business or leap, and for the industry and people you're committed to serving.

Step 5: Craft Your Game Plan

Lastly,, it's time to craft your game plan. Your game plan for skill acquisition is which specific skill you're going to focus on, how you're going to do it to provides yourself with crystal clarity so there's zero chance you get distracted. Often, people approach skill acquisition aimlessly, only to wonder why they're not improving while others, who started much later than they did, are seeing incredible growth.

Your skill game plan involves:

Focused practice time

The concept of deliberate practice by performance researcher Anders Ericsson has been beaten to death, for good reason. It *works*. What makes deliberate practice different from, say, normal practice? Intent, focus, with an outcome in mind: to get better and increase performance.

For example, it's different from picking up the guitar and playing the same chords you've always known over and over again. (This is me, FYI.) This is how most practice: repeating the same patterns. Deliberate practice is staying focused when you're learning a barre chord, your fingers are *killing* you, and your mind wants to quit. Not only does it want to quit, it wants to smash the guitar Kurt Cobain style and leave the room in a blaze of glory.

In other words, it's not fun or comfortable. You're being stretched to your limits, and this is where *real* learning and growth happen.

Studying and learning

Second, you're going to be studying hyper-specific content taught by experts associated with your skill. This is quite different from seeking general information, and your goal is to get *vertical*. Meaning, you're going to go deep. For this, ensure you've strategically chosen content (books, podcasts, academic texts, videos, etc.) in line with your goals.

Hiring someone above your level

Last, hiring someone for feedback on your skill is crucial to success. The right person will be a notch or two above you. They'd have the skill proficiency you're looking to acquire. This is the person who gives you powerful feedback along the way and is worth their weight in gold. Without this last piece, it's very easy to give up long before we achieve breakthrough.

Let's explore two simple examples for clarity on this process:

SKILL: Public Speaking

1. How to talk like TED book, steal-the-show book, online course.
2. Every day, ship one piece of content in the realm of speaking (speaking itself, video/audio, etc.).
3. Enroll in a local Toastmaster's speaking organization with a weekly meeting and direct speaking feedback.

SKILL: Copywriting

1. Online copywriting email course where you handwrite sales letters.
2. 500 words of copywriting every single morning.
3. Hire a copywriting professional for feedback and submit your best work to be evaluated.

Seem like overkill? *Good.* Skill acquisition can easily be put off, because you're not going to feel like it every single day. You're going to want to skip it. Those who become the best in their field strategically acquire new skills or shape the ones they already have time and time again.

Putting It All Together

At this point, we demystified the conventional wisdom of purpose and passion. You should be feeling clear, confident, and ready. We've also identified what you're uniquely better than most at, and how to showcase this value to the world. Remember: although this conversation usually only occurs in the context of business, knowing this is crucial to *any* of your leaps.

Armed with this knowledge and focus, it's time to craft the vision for your leap and never look back.

Chapter 7 Key Takeaways

- **Light your life on fire.** The two crucial ingredients are your purpose (and the vehicle of delivery for it) plus your passion(s). Without these, you won't cultivate the enthusiasm required to stand the test of time.

- **Craft your one-liner.** Clarity on how you deliver your value to the marketplace is everything. If you're not clear, how can you expect them to be? Be bold and specific.

- **Mastery creates value and meaning.** Although purpose and passion are crucial, skill acquisition and the pursuit of mastery are unparalleled for results and meaning.

CHAPTER 7 LEAP POWER STEP

Complete all of the above, including: identify your purpose statement, the vehicle of delivery, your one-liner and your skill game-plan. Be intentional and hyper specific.

_____

_____

_____

_____

_____

Notes

1. https://www.youtube.com/watch?v=5MgBikgcWnY.
2. http://buildingastorybrand.com/minisode-1/.

Chapter 8

Crafting the Vision

T yler Perry needed cash desperately. He had put on his first play in Birmingham, Alabama and urgently needed to rent a van. So, he did what most audacious and broke 20-year-olds would do: he used his mother's credit card. His plan was to repay her with what he made during the performance.

The only problem was it didn't make *any* money. It was a complete and total disaster. Coming home with his tail between his legs, he had to tell her. He couldn't afford to pay her back for the rental. She was livid:

"You *never* gonna make it, Junior," she said. "You need to stop thinking about those plays. Just go get yourself a job with the phone company. Get those benefits."[1]

At this point, most would have taken her advice.

And yet, he persisted. Coming back to his mother, he said, "That's not my life," he told her. "I have dreams. I have more than that inside me." As she responded, she took a long drag of her cigarette, saying again:

"Well, you're never going to make it."

The Voice on the Inside Must Be Loud

Tyler Perry persisted for one reason: **the vision on the inside was bolder than any of the opinions on the outside**. Including the vision from his own mother and the marketplace. Despite endless failures, he kept his eyes on the prize and nourished all the ingredients he would need during his leap. He is now the creator of 19 released feature films, more than 15 stage plays, nine television shows, and a *New York Times* bestselling book.

But it almost *didn't* happen. Perry put every last cent into producing his play, *I've Been Changed*, including renting out a 1,200-capacity theater for opening night in Atlanta. He used his rent, food, and utilities money and put it all on the line.

Only 30 people showed up. Perry was devastated and newly homeless.

After seven years of rejections, empty theaters, and endless bills acting as a reminder of how it *hadn't* happened yet, Perry was ready to quit. He'd decided it was time to heed his mother's advice and apply for a position at the phone company after all. Because of the benefits, right?

It was at that time that two business partners approached him to perform one more time at Atlanta's *House of Blues*. It was March 1998, and one of the coldest nights in Atlanta, and the heater was broken inside the theater. Not *again*, he thought.

And yet, people waited patiently outside to enter a frigid theater and the show sold out. Rapidly gaining attention, he was able to fill two more shows at the 4,500 capacity Fox Theater. He expands:

> Every national promoter I had spoken with during the past
> 7 years, everyone who had turned me down, now had offers
> in hand to take me on tour. Before long I was playing arenas
> with 20,000 seats and filling every one of them.

Approach Tyler Perry Studios in Atlanta these days, and you'll find a sprawling empire resting on 330 acres, bigger than Warner Brothers' studio and Disney Studios combined. Near the lobby door is a simple yet poignant message: *"A place where even dreams believe."*

And that's exactly what your vision for your leap will do for you: point you in the right direction when it seems easier to take the safe path and give up. When your circumstances and the people around you are telling you to retreat, to give in and get real.

The truth is it didn't make *sense* for Perry to keep going. Giving up after seven years is no small feat in itself, but he kept going for one reason and one reason only: **he had cultivated an unshakeable belief in his vision.**

Leap Tip: Detach from Feedback

There are real consequences to dreaming and living boldly. Sometimes, you'll receive feedback from those who gave up on their dreams, telling you to give up, too.

When people close to you tell you that, remember: their intention is usually *good*. Feedback is simply feedback, and you don't have to listen.

Be careful about listening to people who gave up on their dreams. You don't have to give up on yours.

Plant the Seed and Let the Universe Do Its Thing

Without a vision for your leap, you won't persist. You'll experience your first challenge as proof it's not going to work. You'll listen to people's advice to *get real* and to play small. It'll be an exercise in futility and you'll say creating visions doesn't work.

Consider your vision a seed you plant in the ground. This is step one, without the seed the farmer will never be able to experience the gifts of the harvest. So often, people skip past this step, or do it half-hearted. They get a *little* excited, and yet craft a vision lacking any specifics and wonder why it's not happening yet.

Vague visions lead to vague results. Much like the farmer, your vision is the moment you plant your seed. But it doesn't end there. Every single day you're going to tend to the vision to give it the highest chance of flourishing. Although the seed gets water, sunshine, and ingredients in the soil, your vision will *also* get key ingredients designed to make it your reality.

This, in turn, starts to create the conditions you need to bring it to life. There's a moment where all the conditions come together, and *it* happens. For Tyler Perry, it took enough failures, financial loss, and sleeping in cars to have the conditions be *just* right.

I'm not here to tell you it's going to take the same hardship for your leap. But being able to release the pressure and understand there are things happening *for* you, and not to you, can make all the difference in the world.

#NotesFromTheLeap

Tara Mackey, CEO, The Organic Life
#1 Bestselling Author, Singer-Songwriter, Activist

What's the boldest leap you've ever taken and why was this important to you?

In 2011, I attempted to take my own life. This was after a series of tragedies: a tumultuous childhood being raised by a single mother who was a drug addict, and then being taken in by my grandparents. By the time I was 13, I was put on my first drug and by 24, I was on 14. After my best friend's suicide in January of 2011, I was at my wits' end. Working a job I hated in a city I felt unsafe in, with friends and a relationship that was terrible for me. I didn't see another way out. But when my attempt failed, I knew in that instant it had failed for a reason. That I had made a ton of mistakes in my life, but I was *not* those mistakes. I was divine, and as long as I made better choices next time, I could have a better life. Better choices would turn into better actions. Better actions would turn into better habits. And better habits would turn into a brand-new life.

What did you feel as you made this leap, and what happened after?

I felt excited. I went from feeling defeated mentally and feeling exhausted by the next moment, to feeling energized and excited by the next moment. Every moment became an opportunity.

Looking back, what would you tell someone else in a similar circumstance knowing what you now know?

Don't give up. You're not broken. The world has a powerful place for you. The journey is in the hard moments. That's what makes you who you truly are.

Vision Boards Don't Work, or Do They?

Vision boards don't work, life coaches are a scam, and Tony Robbins is simply stealing people's money with a combination of *feel good* energy and a big upsell. If you believe this, then, guess what? It's true.

Every December, my fiancée Taylor and I make a big trip to Office Max and stock up on paperboard, tape, and scissors. We create a vision board experience together, putting up pictures and printouts of the life we'd love to create. We've done this since we started dating, and now create an individual vision board and one as a couple.

It's almost chilling to see how much of the vision board has come to life: a fairytale engagement, a trip to the beautiful northern coast of Spain, a brand-new dream home, a publishing deal, the growth of our businesses, speaking opportunities and much more.

No, I'm not here to brag; I'm making a point. All of these tools *work*, if you work them. Your beliefs will shape the effectiveness of any tool. The reason why the vision board works is because of our belief in it, not the other way around.

In the following section, I'll expand on this concept, but before we get started, I'm going to ask you to wipe your slate clean.

You're going to let go of any beliefs about creating a vision that has held you back. Either a belief that thinking *too* big is bad, or the reminder that last time you did this, it didn't work out. Either way, you'll be right. And I want you to be right in the most powerful way that leads to a transformation during your leap.

Crafting the vision for your leap will involve five essential pillars to ensure it all comes to life for you, in ways that leave you in complete and utter awe.

Vision Pillar 1: Relentless Clarity

The first pillar of your leap's vision is to seek clarity and be relentless with your pursuit of it. Lack of clarity is responsible for keeping people stuck. If you don't have clarity, then what's the point in getting started—*right*?

Wrong. The paradox is, if you sit around and wait for clarity, you'll have less as time passes. On the flipside, if all you do is act aimlessly without any end goal, you can find yourself spinning your wheels with no direction. Like anything, there's a sweet spot in the middle.

Clarity grows as *you* grow. Earlier this year, I spent an entire day at my office planning out the year and all the parts of my business and life. I had an entire whiteboard filled with where I was, where I was headed, and the specifics on closing the gap.

I remember taking a moment and realizing if someone had shown me all of this a couple years earlier, I'd be *beyond* overwhelmed. I wouldn't have done anything. Now that I had grown myself and my business, it made sense. In other words, I had earned my clarity.

To maximize your clarity with your leap, here's what you're going to need:

- **Clarity around your leap's vision**. You must be able to take yourself to *that* place where your leap has happened by asking: *What does your leap look like?* Go deep into the specifics: create a clear picture of every part of your life.

- **Clarity around your leap's feelings.** We don't chase dreams for the sake of dreams, it's about how they make us feel.
  What does your leap feel like? Take yourself to the other side of the leap, and the feelings it brings to you.
- **Clarity around your leap's reason.** Dig deep and identify *why* your leap is something you can't not do.
  Why is your leap so important to you? Why is not taking the leap no longer an option?
- **Clarity around the cost of not doing it.** Identify the tangible and intangible costs of not choosing your leap.
  What does not take your leap really cost you? Why is right now the time to bring it to life?

I use the world relentless for a reason: clarity *never* truly ends. It's a constant pursuit on your path. This allows you to take the pressure off figuring everything out today and instead, start now.

But you can also have all the clarity the world has to offer, and it won't matter if you don't cultivate a belief so deep it courses through your veins.

Vision Pillar 2: Undeniable Belief

Tyler Perry's story earlier was an example of a deep, undeniable belief even when all the external circumstances were saying it was *over*. So was Lisa Nichols, and the stories we've detailed to this point, and in the *#NotesFromTheLeap*.

You will have to cultivate a level of belief that others will deem insane, crazy, or downright out-of-your-mind. That's okay. Take that feedback as proof you're on the *right* path. The second crucial ingredient required to not only bring your vision to life, but to also ensure it happens fast. It all starts with believing in yourself— believing you are not only worthy, but also capable of bringing your dreams to life. Tyler Perry's story is an example of undeniable belief. He expands:

> You have to know it beyond knowing it. It's a feeling inside of you that will not allow you to let go. It will keep you going when you can't keep yourself going. There comes a time in your life when your dream takes on the belief for you, because you can't do it by yourself.

Remember, belief is binary. You either believe with every part of who you are, or you don't. And much like clarity, you'll develop a practice to cement your belief. There's no better way to do so than to collapse reality and take action now.

Vision Pillar 3: Consistent Action (Collapse Reality)

There's a version of me that's 40 pounds overweight. He wakes up sluggish, tired, and hating what he sees in the mirror. He lives in New York City and has been divorced. He's disconnected spiritually and lives in a state of frustration, seeking happiness through alcohol and gambling. He's broke but in ways that transcend paying the bills. He feels a lot like John from Reddit.

This is a *real* possibility. If I had only made a certain sequence of choices, I could be living that life right now. At any moment, there are infinite possibilities you and I could be living, all based on the *actions* we take, or don't.

Think about it this way: there are endless train tracks you and I can choose to get on, and they all lead to vastly different places. Now, today's decisions may not seem like much, but you look out the window of the train and you're in the same spot as the other one—nothing's changed, right?

Wrong, because as time passes, there's a fork in the tracks and everything has changed. Much like my earlier example, there's a reality right now where you've achieved everything you've ever wanted and are living the life of your dreams.

Action, then, becomes the third pillar for bringing your vision to life based on the decisions you make *today*. However, the conventional wisdom around action is based solely on increasing input, with the expectation outputs will increase. Here, we're about something much more powerful: intentional action, rooted in clarity, and belief. When you operate from this place, you collapse the time it takes to bring your leap's vision to life.

Act as If (Your Future Self)

What would the future you do—the one who made the bold decision, took the leap, and brought their vision to life?

This question is one I use every day for myself, for clients, and for my platforms. Because the truth is, the amateur makes decisions *today* based on who he or she has been, which creates a predictable future (rooted in the past.) In that place, the best-case scenario is incremental results, a percentage here or there. Often, this leads to a feeling of stagnation.

The professional operates with a different framework. **Using the question just posed, they make decisions *today* based on who they're *becoming.***This breaks the $A + B = C$ linear model and introduces the $A = C$ model of reality. Figure 8.1 illustrates how this works.

This is where 99% of affirmations, manifestations, dream-of-the-million-dollar-check-and-it-will-come mentality fail. Not only does it fail, but it also leaves people hoping and wishing for handouts that never come. And the reason is simple: they're out of alignment, and the universe knows it. Deep down, they know it, too.

If your clarity and belief are pointing in one direction and your behaviors aren't, you're only going to get so far. Often, that place is one where we believe a little, but because the results don't come (and our actions

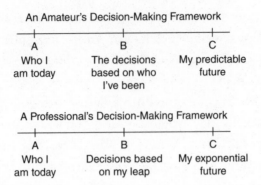

Figure 8.1   Framework for making decisions about your future.

don't collapse reality), we quit. We blame everyone except ourselves, only sending more negative energy toward what we said we wanted.

This cycle repeats itself, until it's over. It didn't work, everything's a scam and you spend the rest of your life analyzing YouTube videos by Tucker in Idaho who's convinced the government chose his patch of land to conduct alien experiments leading to the end of the world and zombie apocalypse.

Okay, I'll admit: I got a little carried away there. Collapsing reality and becoming the future self now is a decision you get to make today. If you sustain long enough, you too will wake up one day and realize you're a completely different person. You walk differently, and you see the world with a fresh set of eyes.

But again, I could be 40 pounds overweight, hating my life. It works both ways.

Vision Pillar 4: Intense Focus

The greatest currency in 2018 isn't cash. It's not followers. It's not Bitcoin either. (Sorry to burst your bubble.) It's one thing and one thing only: *focus*. In a hyper–distracted world, focus is rare. And what're rare is valuable. According to a study on attention spans and focus by Microsoft in 2017, the human attention span has dropped from 12 seconds to 8 seconds.[2]

Sitting 9 seconds ahead of us are goldfish. Yes, we're now less focused and able to keep focused than your niece's little friend, *Nemo*. This finding is damning, and it's only going to get *worse* as technologies invest billions in finding new ways to steal our focus.

I've spent a lot of time inside seminar rooms where people proclaim a massive vision or business idea, and in the moment, they're full of clarity, belief, and even aligned behaviors. But there's one thing missing: intense focus that stands the test of time. Not for a month, not for a quarter, but focus that *endures*.

Leap Tip: Airplane Mode

Make your ability to focus nonnegotiable. Every day, start your day on Airplane Mode with your smartphone. Get used to starting your day with space and focus on the *one* action that would mean you've won the day, even if nothing else got done.

During this time, you're focusing on *you*. Because what most people do is wake up and tend to everyone else's needs and wonder why they don't have any energy left. To build the habit, start with your *first* 45 minutes of your day and expand from there.

So, how do you bring this focus to your life? The good news is that you're doing most of the work. A lack of focus is usually a result of having minimal clarity on one's path. Because of this, distraction becomes a way to soothe the pain of lacking priorities in our lives.

Vision Pillar 5: Cultivating Patience

If focus is rare, patience has become obsolete in a want-it-now world. People expect results *yesterday* and give up the moment they don't come fast enough. This is good news for the right people, those who are committed to play the long game. Consider patience your competitive advantage.

You may be wondering how long this is all going to take. The reality is no one can provide that answer, but you can control key ingredients: clarity, belief, action, focus, and patience toward your leap and vision.

Growth in any endeavor is never predictable. It's not linear, and some days you're going to feel you've got a rocket launcher strapped to your back and other days you'll wonder if it's ever going to work out for you.

What matters is what you do on the days when you feel things aren't working. Often, people let these days become weeks, then months, until they give up. The great tragedy of it all is that they may bow out just before the moment of their big breakthrough. Life has a funny way of testing us *one last time* before we get to harvest.

Stay in the game long enough, and you'll reap the rewards of your patience.

Vision Pillar 6: Total Surrender [–$137.67 Available]

I'd accomplished my *leap* and made the bold decision to move to a place where I knew no one, a place where I felt called for the opportunity to build a life from scratch on my own terms. Even getting to this place had seemed impossible, and yet here I was, living the vision I'd created in my mind on that 13-degree, last-day-of-December night.

Still, the dull screen on my smartphone was painting a vastly different picture. I'd pulled over to the side of the road with the fuel marker beyond empty. I needed gas bad and was 25 miles from home.

CARD DECLINED. Must be a mistake, it has to be.

CARD DECLINED. Okay, well…you know, technology is sometimes erratic, so one more time.

CARD DECLINED. Shit, this is real.

What is happening!? As I pulled up to the banking app, I felt a sinking feeling in the bottom of my stomach.

Current Available Balance: -$137.67.

Here I was: exposed, without the ability to put any gas in my car and an empty fridge at home.

For a few minutes, I sat there trying to come up with a solution. Finally, I had a moment of clarity. I felt alive with a mix of empowering hopelessness and complete surrender. I started laughing and soaked in the moment. I vividly remember telling myself, "This is nothing, and one day you'll be writing about this moment."

Now I am. With no options besides asking people for spare change, I put my favorite tune on and kept driving. The car rattled as every last drop of fuel was used, and that's when I heard the unmistakable clinking sound of a PayPal deposit: "You've received $797.00."

Exhale. I smiled as I pulled off the freeway and found the closest gas station in a state of bliss: I'd made it one more day. Call me crazy, but I didn't believe, out of all the possibilities for when I'd get paid by this particular client, it would happen less than 11 minutes after I'd smiled in a state of complete and utter surrender. There was a beauty to all of it, and you too will have to harness the power of surrender during your leap.

Hopefully, your circumstances will be a little less dire.

Your Vison Is Your Compass

Just like I did on that ice-cold New Year's Eve, you've detailed a vision for your leap. At this point, you should have specifics on what it looks like, what it feels like, and *why* you can't not do it. If you haven't, read this chapter again and make sure you're clear. **If you're vague and unspecific with your vision, you can expect vague and scattered results.**

If you're feeling nervous, *good*. Often, we lose the power of our visions when we start to focus on the how. We tap back into our heads and start to find all the reasons why we're not capable.

Catch yourself. Every time you do, go back and remind yourself of the vividness of the vision. When I woke up on New Year's Day after creating my vision, all I needed to do was to check my phone to see a powerful reminder—a picture encompassing the vision I'd created the night prior.

Armed with your vision, you'll now have a stable foundation as you reach the threshold point of your leap's moment.

Chapter 8 Key Takeaways

- **Your leap's vision becomes your compass.** Without a powerful vision, you'll succumb to the outside (and internal) voices telling you to stop.
- **Clarity and belief grow as you do.** These are not one-time deals; these must be practiced, cultivated, and repeated daily. As you grow, they will too.
- **Embrace the five vision pillars.** Clarity, belief, patience, focus, and surrender are the crucial ingredients designed to bring your leap to life.

CHAPTER 8 LEAP POWER STEP

Craft the vision for your leap. Allow yourself to go to big places, and ensure it comes from the heart. This is not a time to focus on the how: focus on the what, and the why. If it doesn't get you emotional or nervous, repeat it until it does.

_____

_____

_____

_____

Notes

1. https://www.penguinrandomhouse.com/books/534121/higher-is-waiting-by-tyler-perry/9780812989342/.

2. http://time.com/3858309/attention-spans-goldfish/.

Chapter 9

Embrace Your Moment

Standing on the edge of darkness, it was *time*. His entire life had been a lead up to this moment. As he released the last harness, he took a pause to take it all in. It had been five grueling years in the making. Several times, quitting would have been easier. Knowing the world was watching, he delivered his final message:

"I wish you could see what I can see. Sometimes you have to be up really high to see how small you are. I'm going home now."[1] And with that, Felix Baumgartner took the leap of his life as he tumbled from 128,100 feet down to Earth in a dizzying freefall.

You, too, will have your moment. How it looks will differ, but you'll know it's your *moment* by the way it feels. It's a blend of inspiration and fear surging through your veins, and you've never felt more present.

You're in a transcendent, flowlike state where you know exactly what you need to do. You've got a direct line to your future self, knowing the waiting is done. You feel a rush of inner peace. You're doing *it*. After all the talk, all the tapes playing in your head about what to do, or not to do, none of that matters anymore.

Chronos, Kairos, and the Feeling

The ancient Greeks had two definitions of time: *chronos*, meaning the familiar and linear passing of time—past, present, and future. Once the present turns to past, it's gone for good. *Kairos*, another Greek construct, was entirely different; it's about "supreme" moments. These moments are soaked in opportunity and are about seizing them, or else they may be missed forever.

And that's exactly what you'll need to do for yours, because your moment is transformative. It's the crossing of the threshold and taking the call to adventure. It's the moment where everything has changed.

The moment is one of my obsessions. I live for exploring what happens in this split second of time, when we are compelled to choose ourselves in a way we've never done before. With all the incredible guests I've hosted on the Academy podcast, I'm always pulling at the strings of their moments.

So, what exactly happens in your moment and how will you know you're in it?

In the moment, you have a level of clarity you've never had. You can't remember the last time you felt this way. This clarity represents an inner knowing it's exactly what you need to do. It's a straight download from the universe, spirit, or whatever-you-may-believe. It's pure, life-force-energy gold.

In the moment, you're listening to your intuition. You didn't arrive at the moment with blueprints, projections, and P&L statements. In fact, those can't even mix in the same container as the potent energy of the moment. Sure, there is a time for logic, but the way you get to the moment is by tapping into your intuition or what Ralph Waldo Emerson called "the blessed impulse."[2]

In the moment, you don't give a crap about the *how*. When you're engulfed in the moment, the how doesn't matter. What used to bother you and keep you stuck in the past is now a distant memory. You know how the *how* loves to play tricks on you and you aren't having it. No way, not *this* time.

In the moment, there is no turning back and there is no Plan B. When you're in the moment, the other path closed off. It is no longer an option for you. Technically, you *could* go back, but it would eat you alive for the rest of your time here. So, it may as well be dead to you, because there's no turning back and there's no Plan B. Plan B is being relentless in your belief in pursuit of Plan A.

In the moment, doubt and resistance have been replaced by power and momentum. Doubt, fear, resistance, worst-case scenarios are long gone. They've melted off you and no longer exist in the moment. You can't be experiencing both the highest level of clarity in your life and doubt at the same time. It doesn't work.

In the moment, you feel limitless and on fire. The moment is your *Limitless* transition—the Hollywood movie starring Bradley Cooper. In this scene, Bradley's a broke, tired, and half-homeless writer who bumps into an old friend who offers him a pill to help him wake up. He thinks little of it, until he's walking up the stairs, shoulders slumped and apathetic to life. And then, it hits him. He wakes up and sees life through a completely new lens. He notices *everything*. He feels alive. Although your moment may not have Hollywood sets and actors, it'll be just as transformative in the way you *feel*.

In the moment, you've given yourself permission. The moment feels amazing because you've (finally) given yourself permission. You've allowed yourself to declare what you want, even if it's just to yourself. So often, we make halfhearted declarations to ourselves, while we are swimming in doubt and lacking self-worth. Now, you've released the self-imposed shackles and have granted yourself and your dreams permission.

In the moment, you've forgotten all the old narratives. The old tapes of where you failed, messed up, or why your high school sweetheart broke up with you on the evening before prom are nothing but a distant memory. In the moment, you forget *all* these and instead unravel a deeper belief you didn't know you had. Your core essence comes out, because it's who you really are when you drop the baggage.

This is how your moment will feel. Yours is going to look, sound, and be packaged in a way *that doesn't* look like anyone else's. That's the point, because you aren't anyone else. There will never be anyone quite like you. Not living in the period of history you did, with your background, your genetic sequence, and your life experience.

Own it.

#NotesFromTheLeap

Craig Daigle
Fitness Transformation Coach

What's the boldest leap you've ever taken and why was this important to you?

The morning of December 1, 2015 I woke up around 4 a.m. and was choking and couldn't breathe. I was wearing a CPAP machine and being diagnosed with severe sleep apnea and acid reflux; it made for a bad combination. That morning I thought I was going to die. At the time, being a single father, I could think only of my children. I had a legitimate conversation with myself and told myself: "something has to change right now, or your children will be without a father."

What did you feel as you made this leap, and what happened after?

I was terrified. I did my first physical activity immediately following that conversation, and it was the hardest 25 minutes of my life. As soon as I completed it I thought I was going to pass out…fast-forward and I've now lost 130 pounds, I've been cleared of sleep apnea. I no longer take blood pressure medication, I am no longer classified by doctors as morbidly obese. I am a fully active father who enjoys physical play with his children. I have inspired and motivated thousands of others to take control of their health. I've become an entrepreneur and been able to provide for my children as a single father while working full time and taking back my health. It's created confidence and happiness that I only fantasized about.

Looking back, what would you tell someone else in a similar circumstance knowing what you now know?

You are not alone. The life, situations, and circumstances you're living in right now do not define you, and the moment you want to change your story anything is possible.

Other Key Ingredients to Define Your Moment

The moment will come when you least expect it. Although we're going to cover how to *manufacture* your leap, there's only so much you can do. Your moment will be an elegant mix of manufacturing the conditions, while letting the universe do its *thing*. Your moment will come unexpectedly and in a form you didn't quite imagine, which is simply a test—a test of trust and faith, and how open and willing you are to take the next step.

The moment will demand the highest version of who you are. Your moment will demand the highest version of yourself. It will demand you to step into who you really are. Since we've spent so much of our lives relying on external proof in order for us to move forward, this becomes your boldest challenge yet. Your highest self, however, already knows what to do. It doesn't need more validation. It doesn't need approval from others. It's much more powerful than all of that, and it's got your back.

The moment will (soon) seem daunting and impossible. Although you'll feel a sense of energy you haven't experienced in ages, once it's over your moment can seem daunting. Later, we'll cover how to navigate this *gap* where most people get lost in a way that propels them forward. But don't fret, if your moment didn't seem daunting, then I'd argue you're not thinking big and bold enough.

The moment will expose who you really are. During your moment, you're going to be exposed. You're going to face who you really are, and for some, that's incredibly frightening. It has often been said we fear acknowledging the greatest version of ourselves—or even fear ourselves achieving success as much as failure. As the famous Marianne Williamson quotation goes: *"Our deepest fear is not that we are inadequate. Our deepest fear is that we are powerful beyond measure."*[3]

Your moment has the potential to send you on a path you could have never imagined. An experience so riveting, it brings you to your knees. A story so powerful, it becomes an epic in the novel of your life. But what happens immediately after will decide whether you bring it to life or it stays as a movie in your mind.

My Moment (Back in New York)

Back in New York.

Damn, I forgot to excuse myself from dinner, I thought to myself. For a moment, I was deeply concerned for what my friends may be thinking. But then I remembered: I needed space.

Once I clicked the stop recording button, I looked at the timestamp: 4:37. I sat with my legs crossed, my heart beating, and every breath creating a canvas of clouds with the full moon as the backdrop. I sat there, letting the energy of the moment dissipate. I'd made my declaration and faced myself. I was exposed. There was nowhere to hide anymore.

Now what?

I could feel the dopamine slowly wearing off, drip by drip. The lightning strike of intensity was fading, replaced by doubt. The whispers of the *how* started to invade the fortress of clarity I had just created. And I knew, if I didn't act immediately, this entire experience may become a fading memory.

So, sitting on the icy grass, I chose to act. I chose to *do something* to start bringing the declaration to life. But we were approaching midnight and there weren't too many bold steps I could take towards my vision.

But I did *one* thing. I hopped on Google and found it. I found the visual representation of the vision I'd declared moments earlier.

And that simple act was more than enough to cement the experience as real.

Don't Let Your Moment Become a Video Game

The great tragedy of our lives is letting these empowering moments become video games. We experience the vividness of our moment, wake up the next day and don't change anything. Time passes, and our minds find all the reasons to not do it. What I don't want for you is for our experience together and your leap to become a video game. Because no matter how real they seem, they will never be *real*. At least not in my lifetime.

With your moment, it becomes crucial to ensure you do everything in your power to bring it to life. If I hadn't completed the sequence I'm about to share during my leap, this book isn't being written and you're not here.

Step 1: Declare Like Your Life Depends on It

Declaration. Your first step to cement your moment into your life is to declare it with everything you've got. Declare it like your life depends on it, because it does. This is no time to be humble, play small, or use weak language.

Quite the opposite. This is the time you declare your moment, your vision, and your leap with everything you've got. For me, that declaration looked like speaking into an iPhone voice recorder and speaking my truth. As I spoke those words, there was no space left for doubt.

Remember: this is not about being loud or boisterous for no reason. You can whisper and speak in conviction, just like you can yell and not believe it. Find your sweet spot, the place where you're in alignment and speak it into the world.

Leap Tip: Don't Keep Your Dream a Secret

Most people keep their dreams a secret for a reason. Because something magical happens when you declare your dreams—now, they're real. You're on the hook. Within this energy is the power to transform your life.

Now, it's your turn: declare your dreams, or else no one will take you seriously. Including you.

Step 2: Commit with Mind, Body, and Spirit

Commitment. It's time to create a contract of commitment with yourself. This is the moment you vow to not let yourself off the hook. No longer a fleeting memory, this is a life-changing moment.

Real commitment is not simply something you say, it's who you've become. It must transcend and include your mind, body, and spirit. This is full alignment, and a line has been drawn in the sand—a clear before and *after.*

Everything has changed, unless you don't commit. This means you must change who you are on a fundamental level, starting now. Not in a few weeks or when life gets a little less hectic.

You need to start *now.*

Step 3: Execute Immediately or Else

Execution. The third step is to bring your moment down from the clouds and into the dirt. This is where you collapse the gap between your vision and your reality. Often, we believe it must be an act of boldness in the face of deafening adversity.

Although it certainly can be, that's often way too much pressure. Back to my first action: sitting there on the frigid New York night, I couldn't do much in that moment in terms of magnitude, but it didn't matter. Once I'd found the visual representation of my declaration, I set it to become the background screen on my phone.

The next morning when I woke up and was in a completely different emotional state, I was reminded of my declaration. For each of the 77 times I would touch my phone that day, I was anchoring my declaration.

Your action step may not look *anything* like mine. It may be much bolder – saying what you feel during a conversation with your boss, filing the LLC papers for your business, or making the call you've been putting off.

Do it *now* and don't wait one more second.

Step 4: You Are All In, Act Like It

All in. The last part of turning your moment into reality is a complete and total *shift* in worldview, or how you view your place in the world. It's a brand-new lens, and it fundamentally changes the way you experience the day to day.

For years, an explorer was obsessed with finding a new land. He'd stay up for weeks at a time planning his quest, the voyage of his life. Where he lived had nothing to offer him, or so he thought. Years went by until the day of the voyage finally came and he set sail. What he didn't know was the tumultuous storm awaiting him, sending him into a frenzy.

The storm finally passed, and he came across a piece of land: he'd *done* it. He'd found a new world he'd never experienced before. With endless enthusiasm and excitement, he arrived at the shores. Everything was mesmerizing, and he could barely contain himself. His dream was now a reality.

What he didn't realize was he hadn't gone *anywhere*. The storm had shifted his entire voyage, and he'd arrived in a different area of the land he'd known his entire life. What had changed everything was his perspective.

This simple parable is a metaphor for what you're going to experience; it's not so much that everything around you will change, but the way you *perceive* it will.

When you're all in, people feel it. The world feels it, and it'll begin to provide you opportunities, events, people, places, and synchronicities to help bring your vision to life *faster* and with more grace. It's beautiful to watch it unfold, but without harnessing the power of what we've gone through, it won't happen. **Before it comes to life, you better believe it more than anything else you ever have.**

This is what *all in* means.

Unless, of course—you miss your moment.

Leap Tip: Eradicate Weak Language

Language opens up doors to what you and I *really* believe. Often, we use weak and half-hearted language that provides us an easy out and way to blame someone besides ourselves if things don't work out.

It's time to eradicate weak language. Words and phrases such as: *trying, maybe, we'll see, thinking about it, depends, one day, someday, might, etc.*

Instead, step into your most powerful self by practicing clear and powerful language.

Don't Miss Your Moment (It May Never Come Back)

You now know exactly how to identify your moment, and what to do next. The reality is you and I have had countless *moments* in our lives where we didn't fully step in. And while we can look back and rationalize why it worked out, we'll never fully know what one door could have led to.

Don't miss your moment. **This one moment, the way it looks and feels, will never come back to you.** This one is unique and needs to be treated as such. Here are some ways to miss your moment and look back with a heavy dose of regret:

Lack of presence. Presence and awareness are one and the same, and without them, your life-changing moment can pass right in front of you without your undivided attention. Presence is where we mold our experience and achieve a powerful level of clarity.

Lack of courage. Deep down you'll know it's your moment. However, without courage, you won't take the next bold step. Instead, you'll tiptoe around the sidelines. You're waiting for permission. Yet, that very same permission is only granted the moment you choose it.

Lack of trust. Your moment requires a level of trust and faith long before any proof of the result shows up. It reverses the logical pattern of "once I see proof, then I'll step into it." However, that's amateur thinking designed to get you nowhere fast. Masters don't need proof; they create it.

Listening to your inner critic. Any times during your moment, your inner critic is going to be screaming in your ear. *Stop, it's not the right time, get real—this isn't going to work.* We've all heard her, and she's relentless. If you take her word, you'll miss your moment.

Listening to those who don't believe. There are plenty people out there who gave up on their dreams telling others to do the same. Don't listen. Sometimes, these people have great intentions, but it doesn't matter. It may be a loved one, and often it is. It's up to you to move forward no matter what happens.

Tomorrow, Everything Changes

If you don't commit to change after your moment, it will fade. Time will pass, and you'll find more reasons why *not* to do not. When I experienced my moment on that frigid cold New Year's Eve night, I knew I would never be the same. However, when I woke up, I was in a completely different emotional state, with much less clarity. Flipping the phone on and seeing the picture reminded me of the power of the *moment*, and I relistened to the voice note.

For a split second, I doubted myself. But then, I completed these two actions, and they further cemented knowing what I needed to do. By adopting this mindset, you'll cultivate a deep level of trust, knowing it's only a matter of time until your leap comes to life.

Leap Tip: Change Requires Change

Tomorrow, change something. Anything. What matters is that you leave the familiar past that's keeping you stuck. Keep it simple: take a new route home from work, speak up when you'd stay silent, say "yes" to an invite you'd shy away from. This energy rips us from our comfort zones and provides creative energy.

Before moving on, what is the one thing you're committing to changing tomorrow? Keep it simple, and make it matter.

Bridging the Gap

When I left my voice note, I gave myself 12 months. Even then, I felt it was a short timespan to upend every part of my life, but I knew if I made it longer I'd lose the spark. **There is nothing more deliciously satisfying to fear than the passing of time, and logic slowly killing your dreams.**

Fast forward six-and-a-half months, and I'm packing the last of my possessions into a small U-Haul, ready to drive cross-country and begin my quest. Here I was, leaving people I loved, businesses I had created from scratch and the comfort of the *known*.

What I didn't have in bank account zeroes was replaced by ambition, enthusiasm, and the vision I'd crafted. That day, I turned the car on and drove off waving goodbye to my family and the life I'd known.

The truth is, I didn't know what was coming. All I knew was I was giving it a shot, giving myself a chance. And the worst-case scenario was I would come home with my tail between my legs and a *great* story.

Four days, enough caffeine to kill a horse, and a heavy dose of Bruce Springsteen's *Born in the USA,* I'd made it to my destination. Without hesitating, I chose to celebrate the initial journey by taking a hike near my new home. It was sunset, and I was spent from the drive but running high on enthusiasm.

With my heart pumping and legs burning, my breathing was taxed. I took a moment to look up. And that's when I saw *it.*

Forget about a double take, I must have done five. Stunned by its beauty, I unplugged my headphones to get connected and present. And that's when it hit me. I looked down on the phone screen and looked up. Slowly, I raised the phone to match the horizon until it was level.

The purple hazed, sun soaked, Arizona sunset was welcoming me to my new home. As tears flooded down my face, I realized I was experiencing the picture I'd created that night: the same exact shade of purple, with the sun *just* at the right spot with a towering cactus that was just slightly off center.

Just like the picture. And that's when I lost it.

Chapter 9 Key Takeaways

- **Your moment transforms your life.** In this moment, you know exactly what you must do, and you'll know by how it feels.
- **Declare, commit, and execute.** Follow these three principles to ensure you maximize your moment and never look back.
- **Execute now, or you'll miss your moment.** No matter how small the action step may seem, this takes your moment from an experience to becoming your reality.

CHAPTER 9 LEAP POWER STEP

Take a moment to reflect on one time you experienced your moment and didn't act. What stopped you?

_____

_____

_____

_____

_____

_____

Now, take a moment and reflect on one time you experienced your moment and followed through. What did this feel like?

_____

_____

_____

_____

_____

Notes

1. https://www.nytimes.com/2012/10/15/us/felix-baumgartner-skydiving.html.
2. https://emersoncentral.com/texts/essays-first-series/self-reliance/.
3. https://marianne.com/a-return-to-love/.

II

Turning Point: You Will Never Be the Same

This is it. It's what you came for: the transformative power only the leap of your life can bring; the raw, unabashed energy of carving your own path; the sleepless nights, because you're writing the story of your own life. And because it's yours, it's already the greatest story ever told.

As we close out Part II, you now have a powerful perspective on your leap. We've covered it *all,* including how to ensure you have the ride of your life and don't miss it. We've gone deep on how to know it's yours and crafted a vision that compels you.

And now we're at a turning point. If you don't feel ready, then don't flip the page and keep going. I need you present, I need you ready. Because when you flip the page, you are entering into the *unknown.* It's the place where anything can and will happen.

When you're ready, I'll see you there.

Part II Turning Point: You Will Never Be the Same

Out of everything we covered in Part II, what resonated the most?

_____

_____

_____

_____

_____

Why did this specific piece resonate with you? Dig deep.

_____

_____

_____

_____

_____

What are you committed to fundamentally changing for you to integrate the information you've gathered to this point? Be detailed.

_____

_____

_____

_____

_____

PART

III

The Leap of Your Life

The great affair, the love affair with life, is to live as variously as possible, to groom one's curiosity like a high-spirited thoroughbred, climb aboard, and gallop over the thick, sun-struck hills every day. Where there is no risk, the emotional terrain is flat and unyielding, and, despite all its dimensions, valleys, pinnacles, and detours, life will seem to have none of its magnificent geography, only a length. It began in mystery, and it will end in mystery, but what a savage and beautiful country lies between.

—*Diane Ackerman*

Chapter 10

The Business Leap
(Purpose, Unleashed)

Corporate accounts payable, Nina speaking. Just a moment.

In 1999, the movie *Office Space* was released with minimal fanfare. Starring a young Jennifer Aniston, the movie flopped. Years later, it's considered a cult classic and one of the most influential comedies of its time. It's hard to find anyone who hasn't seen it, and the references are endless.

The movie hit it *big* because it connected with a core theme: people's disdain for their work, including the disconnection stemming from a life off purpose, surrounded by people you don't like. It's an over-the-top yet honest look at how we spend most of our time.

And (unfortunately) true.

Often, the biggest, boldest and most impactful leaps you'll ever take will happen with your work. A study conducted in 2017 determined that only 19% of people are fulfilled and satisfied in their work life.[1] I'd say that number is understated, and what most consider satisfied is a low standard to clear. Regardless, the status quo isn't working.

To be fulfilled with our lives, we must feel connected with the value we create for others. We must find meaning and purpose where we spend most of our time and energy. Otherwise, we'll be out of alignment, and find ourselves stuck. This feeling spreads like a cancer to all the other areas of our lives, and then we *wonder* why things aren't working.

The slide to mediocrity with our work is a slow descent starting with taking the safe path others have sold us on.

But it doesn't have to be.

Your Business Leap Will Impact Your Entire Experience

Your business leap is the gateway to unparalleled levels of purpose and meaning. It's the obstacle in the way from you feeling inspired. It's what's holding you back from thinking and being big and bold. Once taken, there is a radically clear before and after.

The before is robotic, routine, and stagnant—the same routines, with the same people every day. There are big promises, yet little to show for them—an insignificant increase in salary and perks, with uninspiring work; a lack of challenge, and spending more of your energy on politics and busy-ness.

Your after is a sense of autonomy and freedom. You're in a place of *thriving*. You experience fulfillment that can't be found when you live another person's vision. You have vigor for what you do, and you're excited about the journey. It's not something you want to avoid, it's something you can't imagine not doing. When it's hard, you don't care. It's the first thing you think of in the morning and the last thing you think of at night.

When you hit this state, it's what Warren Buffett refers to as *"tap dancing to work."*[2] You feel re-invigorated, even though you're on four-and-a-half hours sleep. You smile at adversity, because you've chosen this path. Most importantly, your mindset has completely shifted: You don't have to do anything.

You *get* to.

Specifically, you get to experience the following:

Your purpose is to find your purpose. Your business leap is going to unleash your purpose on the world. As we covered in Chapter 7, your purpose is a driving force. It fuels you in ways that are the greatest source of motivation you'll ever discover.

Your passion will be unleashed. If purpose is the underlying foundation, your passion is the spark that brings it to life. A life without passion isn't a life at all. Passion is stoking the inner spirit inside you that engages you in work with energy, curiosity, and creativity.

You'll have complete alignment in your life. Instead of separating life into convenient categories, your leap becomes an integrated experience. There's no clear separation between your work and who you are; they're one and the same. Your business vision and mission become your guiding lights and put you in a state of connection—with yourself, with what you do, and with others around you.

This is simply an energy you bring where your thinking, your language and your behaviors all function like the separate ridges of a key to create alignment (see Figure 10.1). However, if one ridge is off, there is no amount of force you can use to open the door.

You'll harness your zone of genius. Your zone of genius is what makes you you. It's the aspects of your business or career that no one can do as well as you. They make you feel alive, and you love doing them. There are only two to three key actions that fit the zone of genius, but often we end up doing 23 things—leaving the scraps for what's important.

You won't want to escape or retire. When you're doing what you love, you won't want to escape. In fact, you'll look forward to coming back to your work as much as going on your two-week Greek-islands vacation. Retirement is something you don't even consider, because you know you'd lose what makes you tick. Your leap creates this connection to your work with a palpable energy your clients, employees, and peers can feel from miles away.

You'll be creating lasting impact. In this place, you're at your highest ability to create lasting impact. Before your leap, you realized you were doing very little to impact others. If you're truly an entrepreneur with a business designed to shift others' lives, but you are spending your waking hours doing Excel spreadsheets for your boss in a corporation instead, you're not maximizing your talent, skill, and desire for impact.

You'll have the opportunity for financial prosperity. The ability to create financial freedom is significantly increased in entrepreneurship. A recent study showed people who own incorporated businesses earn about 50% more than people with regular jobs.[3]

There is no doubt your business leap has the potential to change every part of your life. It'll change your perception, your vitality, your energy and the way you engage in relationships. But you'll never know if you don't first release what's in the way and create urgency. Otherwise, the potential to be anchored to the illusion of safety can and will hold you back.

And sometimes, that anchor becomes too heavy to let go.

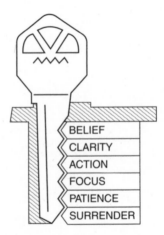

Figure 10.1   The key of alignment.

#NotesFromTheLeap

Shannon Graham
Founder, Shannon Graham Consulting

What's the boldest leap you've ever taken and why was this important to you?

Creating my Legacy program, a $150,000-a-year coaching experience for those who want to achieve the impossible. I was playing small and my value was attached to things separate from myself. In order to expand, I knew I needed to take the leap.

What did you feel as you made this leap, and what happened after?

I felt exhilarated and alive. I was feeling a deep sense of freedom, a sense of power that [made me feel] my reality was totally within my control. After, it took my income to unprecedented levels. Beyond that, it took my identity and impact in the world to unimaginable heights.

Looking back, what would you tell someone else in a similar circumstance knowing what you now know?

Whatever you feel is beyond you is actually the beyond within you. Make the leap; God wouldn't call you to a game you can't play.

The Strongest Anchor Out There

None of us wakes up from our nightly slumber, starts clapping and says, "I want to spend most of my time and energy in a place I can't stand, doing work with little meaning while I put all of my dreams on the back burner labeled '*someday*.'"

And yet, how often do we find ourselves there? The strongest anchor we'll ever experience is our work. It gives the illusion of safety and the world tells us we should be grateful for *even having a job*. Phrases like *it could be worse* start to take over and we cling to something we never wanted in the first place.

Now, I'm not saying there isn't a time to hold steady. But often, the adaptability of the human condition to (painful) circumstances becomes our predictable downfall. In other words, early on you and I can feel pain and discomfort, such as knowing our current jobs are slowly killing us. **But time has a funny way of making the painful more tolerable.** Months pass, we make the uncomfortable tolerable; we wake up seven years in the future and nothing has changed.

Worse off, we've missed out on the countless opportunities we could have had if we had only had the bravery to make a bold decision. As we've explored earlier, the cost of opportunity is real in its impact on our lives. Most people already *know* what they have to do.

But they're lacking the courage to make a bold decision to step into their greatness.

The Excitement Test

"Well, I'm going to wait until things settle down, and *then* I'll get started."

I'm sitting in my office in downtown Phoenix talking to my client about launching his platform, and I can't believe the words I'm hearing. He has already declared what he wants to do, and yet he's still waiting.

We've all been there. Knowing something must change and yet we put it off in hopes for some distance future. Not anymore. With my clients, we use a simple test I call the excitement test to figure this out. It comes in the form of a simple question:

Do you wake up excited for your work, or do you wake up with dread? In other words, if I were able to record your inner monologue during your entire morning before you start *what you do*, what would I learn? For many, it reads like the latest Hollywood horror script.

That's all you need to know. There's no need to explain it. You don't need to rationalize it. The excitement test is my preferred question, because it's simple. You can't fake your way out of it. Honor your answer, because too often, people will talk themselves into believing now is not the right time.

However, with great freedom options come *great* responsibility. In a world with unlimited ways to monetize and make a living, which do you choose? You've already done the hard work during Chapters 5, 6, and 7, which has provided you precious insight to know what you really want.

If you want to be able to live your fullest life, value freedom, and want to tap dance to work, you must figure out what you can't not do, and take what most consider an unconventional path.

The (Not So) Safe Path

Robert Kurson was nearly the writer that never was. Being accepted into Harvard Law School is an exceptional feat, and one most would be thrilled to experience. It is the pinnacle of success. And yet, *something* was missing. This was the safe path, carved out with a near assurance to experience a version of accomplishment everyone would be impressed by: full bank accounts, a fancy title, and access to be in the 1%.

Except for one thing. Kurson loathed law school and knew it was the incorrect path, yet he persisted. He talked himself into staying, thinking practicing law would be much more fulfilling than studying it. It wasn't, and to his surprise it was *worse*. Every Sunday, the theme song for the famous CBS show *60 Minutes* would come on. This became his queue; another week is coming. The show became a constant reminder that, come Monday morning, he'd be back at his desk doing work he despised.

Already making six figures, Kurson was destined for the corner office, a partner position, and potentially making millions. But he didn't care, and he needed a way out.

Fast.

He started with a simple process: writing stories in the evenings when he'd come home from a long day. With no direction, he'd write about memories of happier times when he had hope and looked at his future with enthusiasm. He realized even though he had no formal training as a writer, he lost track of time while he was doing it and was halfway decent.

And then he quit.

No plan, no blueprint, and—oh yeah—zero experience being a writer *at all*. He expands:

> After I decided to make this Kierkegaardian leap of faith, I had a realization: I had no idea how to become a writer. But I was certain about one thing: I was willing to starve in order to leave a career I hated in order to break into one I might love.

Trading a six-figure salary and a path etched in gold, he eventually found a job at the *Chicago Sun Times* doing data entry for $23,000. Although it was a fraction of his original salary, he was having the time of his life. He'd taken his leap.

Today, Robert Kurson is an accomplished, two-time *New York Times* bestselling author, who has written for *Rolling Stone, Esquire, New York Times Magazine,* and many more. He loves what he does and is living his purpose of telling riveting stories through the written word. He traded someone else's path for his, and never looked back. He's not only successful in his craft and career, he's inspired by his work as are the millions of readers he's garnered.

Either Create Courage, or Let It Be Created for You

Kurson manufactured his leap by having the courage to listen to his inner voice. Despite the pressure of staying on a safe path, he leaned into what he knew to be true in his heart; this wasn't his path. I encourage you, too, to listen to the voice inside that knows without a shadow of a doubt if you're on the right path in your career. You must be willing to listen to it regardless of the external forces at play. But we're not always this bold.

Sometimes, you won't have the courage to take the leap on your own terms. In March of 2011, I found myself in that place working at one of the largest sports and entertainment companies in the country.

Like Kurson, I hated it too, until one Friday afternoon when a phone call came in.

I glance down—the caller ID shows two letters: HR.

Human Resources never called me and especially not at 4 P.M. on a Friday right before the weekend.

Shit, I think. And that's when I knew: I was a goner. A sinking feeling starts at the bottom of my stomach and all the way up my spine. Stress starts to overcome me. Then I remember—this is what I want. For the past six months, I'd been tirelessly working behind the scenes formulating the plan to launch my own fitness-training business, which was my passion at the time.

Walking down the stairs, I sense relief. I approach the dark conference room and there she sits—my boss's boss, a person I've never met. Before she spoke, I already knew what was coming.

I want the corporate drivel to be over. As she finishes the long-winded, politically correct routine she's practiced hundreds of times, I smile. In the moment, I want to high-five her, but choose to do so virtually inside my mind instead.

That was *it.* I was free, released to the wild. No longer bound by the shackles of the corporate experience. That afternoon, I rushed to Barnes & Noble, plopped open the laptop, and began the process of launching my fitness business.

I'd taken the leap—kind of. The truth is that I didn't have the *courage* to take the leap back then. I'd forced myself to get fired, so I'd be able to rationalize everything with my parents and those around me. Either way, it worked.

Would I rather have made the bold decision in a blaze of glory? Sure, but at the time, I needed a way to give myself permission. We all want to experience the courage of taking our leap, but sometimes we're going to have our backs up against the wall with no other choice. How you get there matters less than getting there.

#NotesFromTheLeap

Brandon Stephens
Founder, Digital Relevancy

What's the boldest leap you've ever taken and why was this important to you?

A couple years ago, I was still doing home improvement for a local business. I'd been fighting with my demons on quitting and pursuing my own venture or keeping the luxury of all that I had achieved. With no cashflow, no paycheck, two car payments, rent, and bills, I decided I was going to figure out how to make my own money. The backlash from quitting blew me away, including my family and girlfriend. Everyone thought I was crazy for it, and that month became the most stressful month of my life. There were points that got so dark, I was unsure of life. I even called both finance companies and sold my prized cars. It was excruciating.

What did you feel as you made this leap, and what happened after?

Terrified, then anxiety. But the truth is that it helped me through all of it. I created a completely digital business helping visionary entrepreneurs take marketing back into their own hands. I have autonomy and complete freedom doing what I love.

Looking back, what would you tell someone else in a similar circumstance knowing what you now know?

Just do it. Don't think. Jump.

Types of Business Leaps

What kind of business leap will you take? They come in all different forms, but with similar results: a radical shift in the way you experience work and share your value with the world including the following:

Business Leap 1: The Career Shift

You've been in the same spot for years, and nothing is changing. You've heard big promises, yet there's not much to show for them. You're in a career that is no longer serving you or you're in the wrong industry. The career leap is exactly as it sounds, making a radical shift and finding more alignment and connection with your work.

Often, people become encumbered as time passes by and the enthusiasm of a new position starts to stale. They witness others receiving the opportunities they were promised, and it's time for a shift. The changing of an environment is always powerful, and tends to increase our energy, vitality, and enthusiasm for what we're doing. In the career shift leap, it's a matter of stepping closer and closer toward aligning with something you truly love.

Business Leap 2: Zero to Launch

You've had a brimming purpose and passion yet you've been waiting for the right time, when it made sense. You've been waiting for someone outside of you to give you permission, which will never come. But then you realize it may be too late. You're launching your business and going all in on you. You're ready to put your skills to the test and have a dream worth pursuing.

This is the zero-to-launch leap where you're able to experience the autonomy of running your own show. Often, we've known what we'd like to do, yet didn't believe we could go out there and not only replace our current income but also achieve a level of financial prosperity we've only dreamed of. Zero to launch is exactly as it sounds and is a leap full opportunity and an abundance of energy and inspiration—although they must be used wisely. We'll explore how to maximize this leap for your success.

Business Leap 3: The Pivot

You're already in the game as an entrepreneur, but you've simply outgrown what you thought was your purpose. As we mentioned in

Chapter 7, purpose is an evolution, and the vehicle of delivery we use to get there can change. Scratch that, it will change.

When our purpose no longer fits, it's time for a pivot. Pivots are as big a leap as anything else. They're designed to re-align you with who you are today, and they can create a tremendous amount of creative energy. They're designed to serve the audience you feel called to serve. Often, people wait to follow through on their pivot until their backs are up against the wall.

What Would I Do and Love Every Day If I Were Failing?

Tom Bilyeu had been *grinding*. Along with his two closest friends, he'd started what was a successful technology company. On paper, everything seemed to be working out. Except it wasn't.

After eight years of pushing the pedal to the metal, he'd had enough. He was exhausted from creating something only for the purpose of getting rich. And that's when he told his partners: "I'm completely miserable. I quit."

He exhaled, not knowing what was going to happen next. To his surprise, they felt miserable, too. What followed came to life by asking a simple question: *"What would I do and love every day, even if I were failing?"*[4] and that led to starting a protein-bar company. The problem, however, was this market was incredibly saturated and owned by big players in the game.

And again, they had zero experience.

It didn't matter. Bilyeu's purpose this time around was personal; he'd seen his mother and sister deal with obesity his entire life. He knew there had to be a way to help people eat healthier, with foods that still tasted great.

The rest is history, and Quest Nutrition grew 57,000% during its first three years, created a new niche of bars, and came to be valued at over $1 billion. These days, it's impossible to meet *anyone* who hasn't had, or at least heard of a Quest bar.

And therein lies the magic of the pivot: knowing full well the expiration date on your career is past due and having the courage to step into something new. Bilyeu's question, much like Kurson's statement, reveals the power of doing something *you* have chosen for yourself. This self-reliance and freedom allow you to detach from the external result, and yet, paradoxically, create a container for that result to come to life.

It's a beautiful thread across all leaps where success comes from the inside out.

Business Leap 4: The Exponential Shift

You've been in the game as an entrepreneur or feel deeply fulfilled and connected to your work and career. Sometimes, a leap is required to create an exponential shift. After years of incremental growth, you no longer feel challenged, which is key for finding meaning in our work and personal growth. Your leap may be this type of shift—a move that re-invigorates your work life.

The exponential shift may look like adding a new product or service, making the key hire you've been putting off, or simply a catalyst to re-invigorate you to create the palpable energy you once had for your business.

Mostly, the exponential shift is exactly as it sounds; you've felt stuck personally and professionally and are ready to move up a level. To my surprise, one of the great challenges that comes with successful entrepreneurs is boredom, although they wouldn't trade their success for the world, they do miss the early days of having their back up against the wall and overcoming what seemed like daily challenges.

The key, here, is to get back to a powerful place of inspiration with a bold move to become the catalyst for exponential growth.

They're Waiting for You

They're waiting for you, but they won't wait forever. The people who are waiting to be served by you, however that may be packaged, are *ready*. But as time passes and you ignore the leap you know you *must* take, someone else will step up to the plate and serve your tribe.

Right now, there are enough people out there who have a demand for what you're offering that could make you the revenue required to take your leap. The median household income in the United States is (a paltry) $51,939. A study published in the *Nature Human Behavior* surveyed 1.7 million people and discovered fulfillment in life happened at the $95,000 a year mark.

I share these numbers with you for one reason: you're much closer than you think. Now, I'm sure you have bold aspirations and those numbers don't do much for you. I get it. I want you to be able to create a level of financial prosperity you've only dreamed of. But I also want you to know your leap is attainable, and there is no reason that you can't feel fulfilled, inspired, and excited about bringing your work to the marketplace while getting (handsomely) paid for it.

But remember: they're *still* waiting. **Not taking your business leap is selfish.** Yeah, I said it: you're only thinking about yourself. You're focused on your shortcomings and your insecurities at the expense of the impact people are waiting for. Next time you think about making an excuse, imagine them out there. **Pick one person and the pain they're going to continue to be in without your product, service, or offering.** If that doesn't create desire to get rid of your excuses, I'm not sure what will.

I find so many wrestling with all the emotions associated with *not* taking the leap. Yet, once they do take it, they recognize the truth: the worst-case-imagined scenario never happened. They're in a place they could have never imagined, and now there are people who are standing up in support of their message. These people are willingly placing their hard-earned attention, time, and money in your hands.

Eradicate Your Excuses ... Start Now

Without meaningful work, we perish. Without a core essence of a purpose, we lose our spark. Without stepping into a place where we add value to the world on our terms, we can't serve at our highest capacity.

Without taking bold, decisive action, we begin to resent ourselves and stay stuck in a never-ending loop of stagnation.

Taking the leap of your life with your business will change everything about who you are. But remember, it won't happen while you're watching Netflix and fantasizing on the couch. It won't happen daydreaming about what *could* happen. You've got to get in the game, and we've detailed the path to get you there.

Often, I'll witness people who have the *spark*. They have a moment of clarity about their business leap and about why the time is *now.* Their energy of possibility is palpable. They're on fire. And then, a few months later when asked about it, they say, *"Oh yeah, that thing. I'm working on it, but it's on pause."*

You and I know how this plays out: it never happens. I'm committed to making sure this doesn't happen to you. Deep down, I know you are too, or else you wouldn't be here. Let's examine some of the most common narratives and excuses you'll use to not take your business leap and instead stay in the same exact place.

Waiting Around for the (Right) Time

You're going to start … *once.* Once life slows down a little, you'll start. Once life becomes less busy, you'll get going. Once the kids grow up a little, then you'll be all in. Once you get that next promotion or big client, then you'll step into it. Once you make an extra $10,000, then you'll take your leap. Waiting for the right time is the most lethal of all excuses. Why? Well, it's a convincing argument and easy to buy into.

Instead, Make a Bold Decision

Make a bold decision. You know the truth: it won't get easier, life won't get less busy, and you won't be experiencing less stress. The right time is created the moment you make a bold decision. **This is when the world conspires to help you and starts to create the conditions to ensure it's the right time.** Because it's the only time you and I have: right here, right now, the six-inches in front of our faces to choose something new.

Using Fake Gratitude

"Well, I've got a good thing going, and I've got the benefits I need." Fake gratitude is when we talk ourselves out of making a bold decision by masking our disdain with cheap and plastic gratitude. Instead of honoring ourselves with how we really *feel*, we say all the right things. We cling on to fake gratitude and use it as a reason to not act. We use it as a way to justify mediocrity, and we know it. We rationalize away our possibility in exchange for phrases such as:

> "It's not *that* bad."
> "Things could be worse."
> "There's a lot of people who would love to be in my position."

This is fake gratitude, and it'll drink every last drop of your leap until it no longer exists, and you cling on to your current circumstances even though you *hate* them.

Instead Show Gratitude

Show real gratitude for what your life is giving you today. Use it to remind yourself how much you appreciate what's part of your life today, while honoring your feelings about wanting to change. Often, people can get confused about gratitude and how to feel (authentically) grateful while deeply wanting to change their lives. I asked Mastin Kipp, author and creator of Functional Life Coaching, about this dilemma during an interview:[5]

> People often think wanting more means negating what they currently have. You can simultaneously be grateful and dissatisfied. Whenever someone says you should be grateful for what they have, they're afraid you're going to change and leave them behind.

Next time you use fake gratitude, simply catch yourself. Remind yourself this is a mechanism designed to keep you in the same place.

Instead, use real gratitude combined with ruthless honesty to compel you to step into your leap *now*.

Making Decisions Based On Who You've Been

Research has shown the average adult makes 35,000 decisions per *day*. Sure, some of these may be as trivial as what socks to wear, but these add up. And if the old adage of life being a bunch of decisions is true, this is a big deal.

However, how are we making decisions and what is our point of reference? This is what distinguishes those who stay stuck, and those who achieve exponential growth with their leap. The difference is most people make daily decisions based on who they are today, or worse—on who they've been. This creates a predictable future: one in which *most* things stay the same. Sure, incremental improvement can happen here, but it's painfully slow.

Instead Look Toward the Future

Make decisions with your leap in mind. Take yourself to the place where not only your business leap has happened, but also where it's been a success of astonishing proportions. Make decisions today based on what that version of yourself would do. Often, I'll find when I do this with myself and with clients, what seem like big decisions today end up being matter-of-fact ones with the future version of ourselves. For example:

> Instead of waiting to make the key hire in your business, you make it today.
> Instead of waiting to launch the new product or service offering, you do it today.
> Instead of waiting to invest in yourself through a coach or mentor, you do it today.

You can see where this goes. And while making these bold decisions will have a powerful effect on your life today, they're also doing something else; they're collapsing your future right in front of you.

This is the quantum model of decision-making: taking a future as a possibility and bringing it down to today. The old model, the Newtonian way, is one of cause and effect, and one of predictable, linear growth.

Business Is an Endless Series of Leaps

Although you will experience life-defining leaps in business and your purpose, they'll never end. At each new level of growth, you'll have an opportunity to take a new leap. This again, will require you to step into a new level of courage and self-trust.

Daunting? Not quite. If you're simply getting started, it may feel that way: but don't fret. Keep your focus on the leap in front of you, and then you'll realize business is a series of leaps. They won't always be *massive* leaps into the unknown, but they can feel as terrifying. But remember: you're here to grow, and if you're not growing, you're going to slowly slide back to comfort.

The biggest killer of results and growth in business is complacency. The moment you and I decide we're in a comfortable place is the moment we begin the slow slide back to mediocrity.

Your next leaps in business will come in *all* shapes and sizes, including the following

Making the Key Hire in Your Business

Early on as an entrepreneur, you operated out of blind passion and faith. It worked, and now you're in a place where growth isn't as fast as it used to be. Furthermore, you find yourself doing *way* too much. This is where the key hire becomes your leap. I've worked with countless entrepreneurs who'd taken the initial leap but were just as hesitant to make the key hire standing in their way.

Whether it was hiring their first full-time admin, operations person, CFO or anything in between, this key hire was the leap required not only to create massive growth but also to get back to a place of freedom and vitality in their business.

And yet, they waited and took *way* too long. They thought they'd need to add the key hire's salary in new revenue, which is reverse thinking. It's playing small, and relying on incremental growth, when the professional realizes the key hire is *exactly* the domino in the way to create an abundance of profits.

In every case of working with someone who needed to make a key hire (including this guy), it came *six months too late*. Without a doubt, the number-one theme that came up time and time again was a variation of the following: *"I wish I would have done this sooner, this is incredible."*

One of my clients, Jeff, realized he wasn't making his key hire because he didn't want to give up control of his *baby*. But his baby wasn't growing, and it was keeping him up every single night riddled with stress. He'd been running successful financial planning firm yet felt stuck. We worked together, got him clear, and he pulled the trigger. We created a deadline for him, a two-week, European vacation. Upon arrival, we talked, and he had concern in his voice. I'd thought it hadn't work out as well or there had been a crisis at home. He said:

"Tommy…I don't know how to say this, but um, I realized I was barely missed. I expected to come home to endless emails and putting out fires, but she (the key hire) and the team not only handled it perfectly, we grew. I've realized I'm needed *less* than I thought."

For a moment, Jeff was a little down, until he realized this was his dream; he now had the freedom he had so long sought out and why he started the business in the first place. All it took was a little faith, trust, and deciding to use the quantum model. Jeff expands:

> The results were so incredible, I'd started to beat myself up for not doing this at least 24 months sooner. What I realized was the future self, the Jeff five years down [the] line would make this hire in a moment's notice. Once I recognized this, everything changed. We've grown more in the last 8 months than we did in the prior four years.[6]

This is the power of making the key hire your business leap and never looking back.

Stepping Away from the "in" to the "on"

Most entrepreneurs will experience a moment where they realize they're spending too much time in the trenches. Because of the all-in approach of launching and growing, it's easy to get stuck and comfortable working "in" the business, instead of "on" it.

In the business means spending your time on the fulfillment of your brand, product, or service. In other words, doing work employees can and should be doing, including details that make the business *run* but don't necessarily make it grow. There comes a point when an entrepreneur must transition to working mostly *on* the business. This is where leverage is created—long-term strategy, planning, and the creation of new initiatives. Without the burden of always focusing on the micro, the entrepreneur is able to stay on the cutting edge.

This transition can be incredibly difficult and is considered a *leap*. On the other side of it is growth, freedom, and powerful creative energy.

Investing in Marketing, Systems, and Infrastructure

With growth in any business, there comes a time when doing the same of what got us here won't get us *there*. This is when leaps are required, and investments come in various forms: marketing, system, infrastructure, branding, and more.

Whether that's upgrading from your home office in the basement to a real HQ or investing in a marketing firm to help you with the big launch, these leaps are essential to endure growth. Sure, it's easier to make decisions once you have more cash to work with, but I've often found the following to be true: when you have something to lose, it can be much more tempting to play it safe.

These core pillars of your business are designed to build a foundation to stand the test of time. Most importantly, they provide stability as the business grows. There's nothing worse than having a business hit it *big,* only to realize they don't have any of the systems and infrastructure to support or fulfill the growth.

Launching a Brand-New Division, Product, or Service

Last, your business leap could come from launching a brand-new offering, product line, or service and further evolving in your marketplace. This is when creative energy thrives on how you stay on the cutting edge, for yourself and for your clients.

On paper, this may seem so apparent you may be rolling your eyes. But how many companies suffer a fall from grace because of their lack of innovation and keeping up with an ever-changing marketplace?

Kodak invented the world's first digital camera in 1975 but were too hesitant to introduce anything except their core product with film.

Blockbuster was king of the mountain until they ignored where the consumer was headed (delivery and streaming) and stayed stubborn with the belief the consumer would come find them.

Borders Bookstores had a massive retail footprint, but failed to embrace the ever-changing landscape of books through the Internet and digital delivery.

I'd be able to fill the rest of this book with examples, but the point is simple: stay on the cutting edge or be left behind. As of 2014, 88% of Fortune 500 companies from 1955 were gone or no longer existed.[7]

And while you may be thinking you don't have a multinational conglomerate with thousands of employees, stagnation and lack of innovation happens in every business.

It's the local salon that doesn't embrace online booking and loses market share to the audience that prefers to make appointments online.

It's the teaching and education platform stuck on the traditional model instead of finding new ways to create experiences for people through digital distribution.

It's the real estate business focusing on the same old referral techniques instead of embracing video marketing to attract high-end clients.

You get the drill: there's always a leap you can create to reach the next level of growth and impact with your business.

Remember, your business leap can and will transform every area of your life. But life is never linear, and it is impossible to fully compartmentalize. That's exactly where the other leaps in your life may actually become the precursor or catalyst to creating a shift across all the others, including business.

Chapter 10 Key Takeaways

- **Your business leap will transform you.** It will impact every area of your life, and you will never the same. But you must be willing to go all in, and double down on your vision.

- **Create courage (or it will be created for you.)** Leverage your circumstances to create a decision today. But if you don't, you may find yourself with your back up against the wall and have no other option.

- **Business leaps never end.** Business is a series of leaps, and there will always be another micro-leap waiting for you. Embrace this, because business becomes a breeding ground for your personal growth.

CHAPTER 10 LEAP POWER STEP

What is the *one* decision you've been putting off in business, career, and your ability to produce meaning and results with your work?

_____

_____

_____

_____

_____

What's been holding you back from making this decision and why?

_____

_____

_____

_____

_____

What are you committed to doing now?

_____

_____

_____

_____

_____

Notes

1. http://www.mentalhealthamerica.net/sites/default/files/Mind%20the%20
    Workplace%20-%20MHA%20Workplace%20Health%20Survey%202017%20
    FINAL.PDF.

2. https://www.cnbc.com/id/49918773.

3. https://80000hours.org/2016/02/what-the-literature-says-about-the-earnings
    -of-entrepreneurs/.

4. https://www.stitcher.com/podcast/wwwstitchercompodcastresistaverage
    /resist-average-academy/e/53209400.

5. https://resistaverageacademy.com/95/.

6. Private interview, September 2018.

7. http://www.aei.org/publication/fortune-500-firms-in-1955-vs-2014-89
    -are-gone-and-were-all-better-off-because-of-that-dynamic-creative
    -destruction/.

Chapter 11

The Physical Leap
(Vitality on Fire)

Rich was like most 40-year-olds: slightly overweight, but not enough to be considered a problem. Sluggish and drained, but that came with the territory, decades of obsessing over a career in law, waiting for a time he could truly *rest*. He was tired, but who wasn't? At least that's what he believed; life is supposed to feel this way, especially when you're pushing to become partner at a prestigious law firm; 80-hour weeks become the norm.

One night after a particularly intense week, he found himself walking up the stairs to his bedroom to meet his wife who was already fast asleep. Not anywhere near the top, he had to rest: he was short of breath and gasping for air. He wiped off some sweat and thought he may be having the start of a heart attack. He looked down and realized he'd only gone a few steps up the stairs of his home.

What the hell, he thought to himself. The years of poor health, a shitty diet, and pursuing success at the expense of his physicality came to a screeching halt. He was not only disappointed but he was also disgusted and embarrassed at who and what he'd become. At age 39, he was staring into the abyss of a brand-new decade, and yet this number represented a special opportunity: the chance to change radically.

Otherwise, he was going to drive his entire life straight into the ground. *Literally.*

That evening, Rich made a decision and experienced his *moment.* He would never be the same, and there was a clear before and after. This was it for him. Rich explains, from his book, *Finding Ultra:*

> Yet in that precise moment, I was overcome with the profound knowledge not just that I needed to change, but that I was willing to change. I'd learned that the trajectory of one's life often boils down to a few identifiable moments—decisions that change everything. I knew all too well that moments like this were not to be squandered. Rather, they were to be respected and seized at all costs, for they just didn't come around that often, if ever. Even if you experienced only one powerful moment like this one, you were lucky. Blink or look away for even an instant and the door didn't just close, it literally vanished.[1]

The next day, Rich didn't simply commit to adding more vegetables to his diet and a new membership at the local Orange Theory Fitness. He became a new person. With no plan, blueprint or experience, within six months he'd signed up for a special endurance event called the Ultraman—a triathlon on steroids—a three-day event, spanning 320 miles on the big island of Hawaii. He finished 111th and began his quest to become one of the world's fittest athletes. In 2009, *Men's Fitness* named him "one of the 25 fittest men in the world."[2]

Fast-forward to today and you can't help but think of Rich Roll when discussing training, nutrition, and healthy lifestyle. He's a pioneer as a vegan athlete, a household name in endurance training, and host of one of the most popular podcasts in the world. His physical leap lead to a complete transformation across all pillars of life: physical, mental, emotional, and spiritual.

And you can do the same.

Who It's For

We live in a world where we chase all types of success at the *expense* of our physical vitality, energy, health, and confidence. Then, one day, we wake up and realize what this Faustian tradeoff has done: left us broke. We're forced to say no to the invite to hike the mountain. We're unable to last playing in the yard with our kids. We lack the energy to do the things we love. But worst of all: or lack of physical vitality and health stops us from creating our dreams. **Big dreams require *big* energy**—often, they don't come to life simply because we're drained.

Ask yourself this: **Do you feel your physicality is a catalyst to growth in all other areas of life or is it an anchor?** For most Americans, the answer is obvious: it's a Titanic-sized anchor, and only getting worse. Three quarters of American men and 60% of women are categorized as obese or overweight, and now our children are suffering.[3]

But even if you don't consider your body an anchor, are you maximizing its potential? Your physicality goes way beyond looking fit at the summer BBQ; what it does to your mind, performance, and creative output is a gamechanger. According to John Ratey, author of *Spark: The Revolutionary New Science of Exercise and the Brain,*[4] exercise creates a pharmacy of chemicals in our brains unlike anything else (including feel-good chemicals serotonin and norepinephrine).

He expands: "*It lights a fire on every level of your brain, from stoking up the neurons' metabolic furnaces to forging the very structures that transmit information from one synapse to the next.*" Like anything else, we tend to ignore our health until the crisis hits—and then it's too late. Here are some ways to know its time for your physical leap:

If you're feeling sluggish and tired constantly, it's for you.
If you've been on the slow path to a health crisis, it's for you.
If you've lost touch with your body as a tool for growth, it's for you.
If you're tired of saying *no* to what life has to offer because of your body, it's for you.

If you're feeling blocked creatively or lacking clarity with your vision, it's for you.

If you want to experience a new level of challenge and perspective, it's for you.

Furthermore, the mental confidence and resilience forged by pushing ourselves physically has a direct carry over to other areas of our lives. Your physical leap can light a blowtorch to your business, relationships, and connection to yourself and others.

Waking Up to a Health Crisis

I was *toast*. My energy is (usually) astronomical in the morning, much to my fiancée's dismay (she wakes up a little slower, or at what would be considered normal). It had been a few days since I had *any* energy, so I went to a vitamin IV drip to pump my body full of vitamins.

It didn't work, and I was out a cool $175. *So much for recovery,* I thought. Things only got worse, so I booked a massage. I couldn't finish it, because the therapists touch affected my breathing and caused pain all over my body. It was unbearable.

This isn't normal, I thought. I'd like to think I know my body decently well, and none of my usual fixes were working. My fiancée had enough, and demanded we'd go to the Urgent Care I said it was a waste of time, but I felt so terrible, I followed through. After a round of tests, they came back with the diagnosis of pneumonia and sent me on my way with some powerful antibiotics.

"Your symptoms should start improving in 72 hours or less." Tick, tock. Time passed, and nothing changed. I only felt like a bigger boulder had stampeded by entire body. I couldn't shower, eat, or breathe. Shortness of breath surrounded my experience, and we want back to the urgent care. This time, they told me: You've got *double* pneumonia now.

Finally, that's when I admitted myself to the emergency room where a test came back with a rare lung condition found in the soil of the dry southwest climate, named Valley Fever. Fungal spores accumulate in the dust, and when breathed in can cause a serious condition. For many, the road to recovery can last anywhere from 6 to 24 months, but symptoms can last forever and spread to other areas of the body.

I was destroyed. For what seemed like weeks, I'd wake up in tears. No energy, and I'd look out to a window of a mountain I used to run up and down freely at full speed. I didn't know what would happen to my business, which required tremendous energy and face time.

My identity was rocked, and I spent hours alone locked in a closet journaling, thinking and meditating. My story isn't unique, except for the fact that at the time I was a healthy and fit 31-year-old whose idea of a cheat meal was farmed salmon. Getting rocked by Valley Fever was rare, and a reminder: **our health will dictate the quality of our lives**. Without it, we don't have much. It was a tough pill to swallow, and the recovery called for anywhere from eight months to a lifetime of symptoms.

If you're out there reading this and have been neglecting your foundation, think again; your physical leap is your opportunity to reverse the damage that's been done. You don't want your health to become the ultimate roadblock to your dreams, and the best time to start was yesterday. The second-best time is *right now*.

A Deeper Reason for a Powerful Result

Regardless of the physical leap you choose to step into, there must be a deeper *reason* behind it. We're conditioned to choose physical goals and outcomes for half-hearted, vanity-laden reasons: look better, lose 15 pounds, and get ready for the wedding. However, these rarely last. Without a deeper *why*, we lose interest a few weeks after we started.

That's one model, and it's not working. Instead, you'll have to develop a reason for your physical leap, one you can lean on during the difficult times. There will be plenty of times when you don't want to train or push yourself. There will be days you want to sleep in. But if your why is strong enough, you won't listen to those voices looking to make sure you play small. Develop your why, and never look back.

Your powerful why may be the way you show up for your family or the people you love. It could be about getting to know who you are and building deep confidence. It could be about seeing what you're made of or setting an example for others.

What is *your* why? As you read through the rest of this chapter, keep asking that question in the back of your mind and don't stop until you feel *it*.

Leap Tip: Big Dreams Require Big Energy

Years ago, I ditched training myself physically for vanity. Sure, looking great is fun, but here's what I know to be true: big dreams require tons of energy. The great news is: once you commit to training for performance, you stop skipping workouts and get all the aesthetic benefits.

Why do you train? Connect your physicality, vitality, health, and energy to your leap and you will never dread a workout again.

What Your Physical Leap Will Reveal

Your physical leap will *change* you. You're going to experience the tangible physical benefits that come with making a bold decision for your physicality, and yet that's barely scratching the surface. When done the right way, your physical leap will create a catalyst effect to open up doors you could have never imagined.

Abraham Maslow is considered one of the most influential psychologists of the twentieth century. In a landmark paper published in 1943, he revealed what drives human behavior and motivation by identifying a hierarchy of needs. Used worldwide, the impact this model has had is unquantifiable.

The core premise is simple: as human beings, we have needs and those needs must be met before we can fully develop and grow into the next stage. If we don't have our basic needs of food, water, shelter, and rest, we can't move on to the higher levels: safety needs, relationship and love needs, self-esteem needs, and self-actualization.

Enter what I call the *Homeless Paradox:* I can go to my local street corner, and find people living there or begging for cash. If I got out of the car and presented them with say, *Think and Grow Rich* and sat them down to teach them the lessons, they (likely) wouldn't care. The information would pass right through them. Why? Because they're thinking about their next sandwich, and how they're going to make it through the pending thunderstorm the same evening.

This is Maslow's hierarchy of needs in practice, and while I'll assume you're not on the street, it applies. For the purpose of your physical leap, the premise is simple: if you're unwilling to focus on your physical growth and needs, it becomes difficult to maximize your potential. The easiest entry for transformation in the rest of our lives is the physical.

Here's what to expect once you commit to your physical leap:

Learning about who you are. There is no faster way to find out what you're made of than pursuing your physical leap. Often, people who I may have mutual connections with or have known through social media will ask me out to coffee. I'll usually defer and come back with:

"How about we meet at [mountain] at sunrise on Wednesday, instead?"
The reason is simple: I want to dig deeper into who this person is and create an authentic connection. Sitting in a comfortable Starbucks in a crisp 69-degree room doesn't reveal character, and we end up barely scratching the surface. No, I'm not a Navy Seal commander. What I want to know is what kind of grit you have when life gets a little hard. It's not about performance, it's about *attitude.* Which is exactly one of the key benefits of your physical leap: you learn a lot about yourself when life gets spicy.

Reconnect with your temple. We get one vessel for this experience and we sure as hell don't act like it. Years of pounding our bodies with caffeine, stimulants, alcohol, sugar, and little sleep have created a disconnection with the most adaptable machine on the planet: our bodies.

The effects of this disconnection are devastating, including: an inability to experience life fully and say yes to all she has to offer. Beyond optimizing your health and ensuring you've done everything to make sure you're here to stay, reconnecting with your temple leads to making better decisions on a daily basis, for example:

You'll be less likely to eat sugar when you're stressed.

You'll be less likely to drink toxic alcohol when life gets hard.

You'll be less likely to wake up with no energy, all while facing a 14-hour day.

Experience countless (life) lessons. Our physicality is a source of endless wisdom and lessons about life. Want to quit when the training session gets hard? You'll do the same in your marriage. Want to shortcut reps and cheat your way to a score? You'll do the same in business. Want the easy path, infomercial six-pack-abs in a week result? You won't endure when you're six months in and still not *there*.

Training physically provides a myriad of life lessons about what it means to develop discipline, persistence, grit, and fortitude when faced with challenge. My obsession with pushing my body to the extreme started from wanting to know a little more about who I was when life got hard. I wanted to see what I had inside, what I was made of, and how I would respond to adversity.

Have the vitality to pursue growth. Finally, life requires a tremendous amount of energy daily. Simply from a physiological standpoint, the amount of energy it takes for your body to keep you alive is remarkable. But that's just square one. Your physical leap will provide the energy and vitality to bring your life's vision and make it real. Often, people are simply held back by not having enough energy to follow through on their dreams.

The Spirit of Kokoro

Mark Divine knows a little something about physical performance. A former Navy SEAL who finished first in his BUD/S class, Divine commands presence at a moment's notice. You can feel his energy from a mile away; this is a man who's been through the fire a few times, and he won't take your *bullshit*.

Upon retiring from active duty, Divine wanted to find a way to bring the lessons, fortitude, and real-world life skills he learned from his experience to the everyday person. He knew the gifts he received from his training were needed today, leading to the launch of SEALFIT, a physical and mental online and in person platform to help people become their best selves starting with intense physical training.

One of these experiences, which Divine aptly calls *crucibles,* is named Kokoro. The Japanese word for heart, Kokoro brands itself as "the most difficult training available to civilians."[5] And universally, it lives up to its title, spanning 50+ hours of hell-week-style training where attendees are pushed to their limits on little to no sleep. No full starting roster has ever finished together, and the pass rate hovers around 30%. But Kokoro isn't simply about crushing people; anyone can do that. What Kokoro does is strategic and designed to tap into something much deeper. During an interview with Mark, he expands:

> Within hours, you realize it's not about the physical as that burns out quick. Without sleep, you are being tested mentally in all types of ways without any solution. With the mental burn out, you get to an emotional place where you dissolve your ego and ask your teammates to help or help them. Once they go through this, the intuitive part of us comes through and you experience powerful clarity and flow. Lastly, you experience the spiritual mountain, or what we call warrior spirit, this is Kokoro. Knowing who you are at the core.[6]

This is the power of a physical challenge and leap: by opening the door, **we get to experience transformational shifts as long as we're willing to dig deep and push what we believed were our limits.** Now, I get it: you may not be looking to experience hell week with Navy SEAL veterans screaming in your face for 50+ hours. Again, it's not about *the size* of the leap, it's about what it does for you.

Types of Physical Leaps

So, which physical leap are you going to take? There are countless options, but here are some common leaps designed to take you to the next level, regardless of where you're starting from today.

Physical Leap 1: The Call to Adventure

One of the most effective ways to create a powerful physical leap is to wrap it around an experience. This can be seeing a part of the country or world known for its vastness and beauty, where you must earn your view. Not only will having a compass of an experience guide you every step of the way, you're able to create a lifelong memory to anchor your leap. The awe and wonder of the experience will determine your level of intensity through the process, and will no doubt create a shift in your perspective and possibility.

What this looks and feels like is up to you. There are countless options available to you. For some, that may be entering a physical crucible similar to Kokoro where you're tested beyond your limits. For others, that may be headed to Mount Rainier and climbing 14,411 feet. The adventure leap in regard to your physicality includes a specific experience, a deadline with a date and time, and a stretch of your (current) physical abilities.

Physical Leap 2: The Radical Lifestyle Shift

The second physical leap is all about committing to a radical lifestyle shift with your physicality and lifestyle. It's Rich's story from being an overweight, out of shape, 39-year-old to turning your diet to plant-based and committing to endurance races. It's deciding to completely revamp a part of your life where there's no way out, and zero chance you'll go back to your old ways.

One of the best ways to create a radical shift is to commit to an everyday practice with your physical leap. Want to start a yoga practice? Commit to 30 days in a row. Want to shift your diet? Throw out all your food and go keto for the next 30 days. While radical shifts require a lot of initial energy, after two or three weeks you'll start adapting and it will become your *new* normal.

Physical Leap 3: Stepping into the Ring

Sometimes, you've got to step into the ring. Figuratively and literally, the third physical leap is about taking the bold step of entering a new arena of sport. One of the best ways to ensure the success of your physical leap is to wrap it around the commitment of a new sport. It's a surefire way to increase enthusiasm, dedication, and find something *new* to invigorate your discipline on a daily basis.

This physical leap could look like committing to a boxing or martial arts practice, a new sport such as endurance running, swimming, mountain biking, or functional fitness and countless others.

This year, I stepped into the ring of the mountain bike world and even though I'd had a decade of physical training, it re-inspired every part of my training, nutrition, and lifestyle. I was having the time of my life while getting in grueling training sessions. This is where you find the best of both worlds: the sport or activity is so fun to you that you don't realize how hard you're training.

Most importantly, you eliminate the constant use of willpower to enslave yourself to the gym and, instead, you are choosing to do something you already like. The key, again, is to truly commit and go all in—which we'll discuss below to ensure your success.

How to Create Your Own

If hiking one of the nation's hardest mountains or stepping into a boxing ring sounds daunting to you, don't fret. I'm giving extreme examples to show what's possible for you, but ultimately, make it your own, based on where you find yourself today, and what feels right to *you*.

What will make or break your physical leap are the core essentials to make sure it sticks. Remember: your leap is not a halfhearted decision in which you throw in the towel after a few weeks.

Let's examine how to ensure your success every step of the way:

Commit or don't start. Unless you're *all in*, don't start. Commitment in this case is binary, and often with big physical challenges or initiatives, people start half-hearted and give themselves a way out. Not here. Once you commit, understand you will have days and moments when the enthusiasm of committing to your physical leap has faded. It doesn't matter, because you're staying committed to your word and following through for much bigger reasons.

Enroll others and build your tribe. Your physical leap will need a powerful foundation of support, urgency, and accountability. Rolling solo, for most people, is a terrible strategy that never lasts. The great news is there's never been more access to hyper-specific communities who are taking all kinds of leaps and adventures with their physicality. Enroll people or join a tribe that will push you when you don't want it.

Choose a date and time to show up. Regardless of your leap, you must have an *event* you're chasing. This event requires you to show up and put yourself on the line. Running a 10K in your local neighborhood on a Saturday morning is quite different from a Spartan beast with tons of other motivated, pumped up competitors in a raucous environment.

Pay, or else you won't pay attention. Investing in yourself for your physical leap will secure your commitment long term. Join a new training facility, hire an online running coach, put down the hotel and guide money on the hiking adventure; paying means you're locked and loaded and much more likely to finish the endeavor. Even if you feel financially strapped, there's always a way to make it happen and secure your (financial) commitment.

If You Do This Right, You May Never Be the Same

There's a physical leap that's been calling you. It's a new sport, adopting a yoga practice, hiking a mountain you've always wanted to, or taking the adventure you used to dream of.

These are always easy to put off until next month, next season, or next year—and we often do, because we need to make money and pay the bills. But remember, your physical leap may be the catalyst holding you back from rapid growth in other areas of your life. I've seen firsthand how a burned-out entrepreneur transformed his or her life and business by enrolling seven friends for a physical leap on a hiking adventure. I've witnessed people radically shift their lifestyle and take a leap into a new sport and practice, leading to newfound confidence and enthusiasm.

It's easy to put off physical leaps, especially if you've been used to putting your health and vitality on the backburner. No more, and you know this is for you if you've been avoiding it—and there's no more looking back. It's your *time*.

Chapter 11 Key Takeaways

- **Your physicality is about much more than looking good.** It provides clarity, mental toughness, resilience, and a myriad of chemicals proven to boost confidence and purpose.

- **Having a deeper "why" will get you out of bed.** Training for vanity doesn't endure; instead, embrace the deeper why and you'll never rely on willpower again and you'll get the benefits from looking great too.

- **Big dreams require big energy.** Without energy, none of your dreams will come to life. If they do, they won't last. Embrace this and take an honest look at your physical and mental energy in regard to your leap.

CHAPTER 11 LEAP POWER STEP

What is the one decision you've been putting off in your body, training or lifestyle to produce clarity, energy, and momentum?

_____

_____

_____

What's been holding you back from making this decision and why?

_____

_____

_____

What are you committed to doing now?

_____

_____

_____

Notes

1. https://www.amazon.com/Finding-Ultra-Revised-Updated-Discovering /dp/0307952207.
2. http://www.vegsource.com/news/2009/11/meet-rich-roll—one-of -2009s-mens-fitness-magazine-25-fittest-guys-in-the-world-and-dedicated -vegan.html.
3. http://www.healthdata.org/news-release/vast-majority-american-adults-are -overweight-or-obese-and-weight-growing-problem-among.
4. http://psycnet.apa.org/record/2008-02933-000.
5. https://sealfit.com/kokoro/.
6. https://resistaverageacademy.com/ep-33-how-to-forge-an-unbeatable-mind -body-and-spirit-with-sealfit-founder-mark-divine/.

Chapter 12

The Spiritual Leap (Disconnect to Reconnect)

Jack Dorsey is a *busy* man. As co-CEO of two massive companies, Twitter and Square, he's got a lot on his plate. He's being pulled in millions of directions, making countless giant decisions every day, and dealing with the intensity that comes with running not one, but *two* major tech companies that run global operations on a grand scale.

And yet, he needed a break. Most of us believe we don't have the *time* to meditate for five minutes, let alone to disconnect from the planet for 10 days. To kick off 2018, Dorsey did just that; he enrolled in a Vipassana meditation retreat, a grueling Buddhist practice where all of one's time is spent in deep, quiet solitude.[1] This isn't your local yoga studio's version of meditation, plush with cushions and a little-too-much Lululemon.

This is *hard*. Hard as in you want to quit. Every part of your body aches from sitting cross-legged for nine hours and your mind is swirling in chaotic thoughts mimicking more of a serial killer than someone looking to acquire presence and Zen. And yet, on the other side of the discomfort is a new perspective on life, work, purpose, and meaning.

Dorsey's retreat was an example of a spiritual leap: taking time to disconnect from the world to tune in to what *really* matters. Here is where baggage is released; obstacles are obliterated; and the mind, body, and spirit are restored. What seemed like a big deal earlier now dissolves, and you operate with a deeper, more grounded sense of clarity and purpose in your everyday life.

The spiritual leap is a game changer and will take you to places you could have never imagined.

If you have the courage to step in, of course.

Leap Tip: Insights Happen When You're Not Forcing It

Take a moment to think of the last idea you had or moment of clarity. Were you in a place of forcing it? In most cases, our ideas and clarity don't happen when we're pounding the pavement.

They happen during the *white noise* of life. It's time to break up with the do more, to be more model. Where can you *be* more, to do more?

Destination Nowhere (Except Inward)

Black Rock City sits in a desolate stretch of desert two-and-a-half hours from Reno, Nevada where *nothing* seems to be happening except intense, swirling dust storms. And yet, every Labor Day weekend, thousands of people descend on this empty stretch of barren desert and create a temporary city and community out of thin air.

At this point, you've (likely) heard of Burning Man: a yearly gathering where the hippies go in the desert to meditate, dance, and do-what-*those*-people-do. Except, the stereotype is gone, and the event attracts people from all over the world, from the tech billionaire to the 19-year-old surfer to the mother of five.

Describing the Burning Man experience is near impossible, as that's exactly what it is: something you must experience. On a superficial level, there seems to be nothing special about the gathering: it seems like a lot of young people partying in the middle of nowhere. I spoke with my friend and two-time burner (the not-so-unique moniker you gain from experiencing it all) entrepreneur and owner of Life Is Rare – Brandon Duncan, to expand:

> Burning Man is another planet ... a vast ocean of dust and art and music and people and so much creative energy ... and then the evening comes, and it feels like a video game turns on and you suddenly know how to code your experience into whatever you desire.[2]

Sounds like a high-school, dream right? Except some of the world's most successful entrepreneurs, artists, business moguls, and creatives make up a large percent of the crowd. Elon Musk is a known participant and credits the gathering with deep insights. Tony Heish, owner of Zappos, is a regular alongside Larry Page, former CEO of Google. Page used it to find his successor as CEO, once he'd found out Eric Schmidt was a burner.

Clearly, there's *something* to it. People can party and dance anywhere and weaning off a hangover is hard enough (at least for me) in a plush Las Vegas hotel room. Try a tent in the middle of the desert.

But regardless of your notions of this gathering, one thing is clear: it *changes* people. It provides a shift in perspective. Connections are made, businesses are born, and life-changing insights are commonplace. A renewed sense of spirit and enthusiasm is brought back to life upon reentry into society. When I asked Brandon to expand on the benefits, he told me: *"I experienced a gigantic shift in the understanding of my personality and why I am the way I am as well as why I do the things I do: both positive and negative, or healthy and unhealthy. This gives me a beautiful opportunity to design a new, more useful approach to key aspects of life such as business or being a father."*[3]

Burning Man, then, simply produces the outputs you'll be achieving with your spiritual leap: clarity, connection, a sense of purpose, and tapping deeper into who you really are. All work synergistically to fuel every part of your life while providing a sense of fulfillment and reflection, which is rare.

Often, you won't find the groundbreaking insight you're looking for learning from someone at a whiteboard. Although this is effective, sometimes it takes a radical shift in your environment to open up a new possibility you *never* saw coming.

And that in itself is worth its weight in gold.

Who It's For

Do more to *be* more, right? The conventional wisdom states we must do and then do some more, and that leads to results. And yet, this is the old model that has left many people with a lot of external markers of success but missing the key ingredient of fulfillment: feeling connected from the inside out.

The truth is: we can fill our lives with all the external objects, shiny cars, and vacation homes and *still* feel empty inside. The story of the entrepreneur, business mogul, or artist achieving success only to feel depressed sounds like a broken record by now, doesn't it? And yet, it paints a powerful reality: if we don't fill ourselves up internally, then our external success becomes fleeting and painfully hollow.

Because achievement and fulfillment don't mix. It's like pouring cement into your oven and wondering why you're not eating a delicious dessert that evening. You may be thinking, well, I'm here to create results, and the book title is about action, and a *leap*. You're right, but there's a stark difference between action for the sake of action and *purposeful action* anchored to a vison (as outlined in Chapter 7).

The old model works; don't kid yourself. Yet, we must define *working.* Because my definition of success never means financial prosperity in exchange for relationships, my physical well-being, and my spiritual connection. The new model, and the one adopted by the uber-successful is the following: be **more to do more.**

No, this isn't about sitting around Indian style in your living room dreaming of a million-dollar check, heading across your driveway, and opening the box only to find the latest Valpak coupons. It's about injecting time *being* into our lives, so when we sit down to create the new marketing plan, we do so with intention and clarity. When we wake up, we're doing it for a reason that matters. Although these differences can seem subtle, they operate on a razor's edge and can create a colossal difference in the quality of our lives.

Who's the spiritual leap for? Here are some ways to know it's for you:

> If you feel you've been on overdrive or aimlessly wandering, it's for you.
>
> If you've been on the verge of burnout, quitting, or giving up, it's for you.
>
> If you want to go from doing to being and achieve a powerful perspective, it's for you.
>
> If you've felt yourself running on fumes too often and wondering how long it will last, it's for you.
>
> If you feel a calling to explore some of the deeper truths of life, the spiritual leap becomes your quest.

It's hard to find someone who can't benefit from a spiritual leap. No matter who we are, we can *all* benefit from some time away. Too often, we wait to have a crisis or life-altering moment to disconnect and go within.

And sometimes, it may be too late.

The Greatest Quest

We're all on a quest with our lives. Joseph Campbell's *Hero's Journey* studied the history, origin, and themes of myths through the ages, culminating in a brilliant summary of key events that are part of every story, countless Hollywood movies, and, most importantly, our very own lives.

The quest, then, is what you're here for. And your spiritual leap is the quest within: back to center. This is why the *result* of the spiritual leap is palpable in people's lives: **it's the greatest journey you'll ever take, and one designed to alter and amplify every part of your experience.**

One of the great benefits of tuning out to tune in is the power of reflection and deeper questioning. After passing the initial resistance of quiet, we're often left with a set of questions we don't have the answers to, but simply by asking—we open up new pathways to discover them. These chart the course of our lives, and give it more depth, vibrancy and color.

But that's not all—far from it. Here's why your spiritual leap can be the most powerful experience you'll ever have:

Leaps break down your reality and patterns. Life can seem monotonous every day, even if we love what we're doing. Often, we don't, only making things worse. Everyone knows what it feels like to be in a *rut*. Nothing seems to change and looking forward to our day seems like a pipe dream. A spiritual interruption breaks our reality and provides a hard shift to our experience. This shift, alone, is tremendous in its lessons and insights.

You question everything (and that's a great thing.) Once your patterns are broken down, you create enough white space to start asking some deeper questions. Often, these questions have been inside us all along; we simply drowned them out. These include:

Why am I here?

What is my purpose?

Am I living my best life?

What am I grateful for?

Where do I want to go?

What am I doing this for?

What is not working?

Through this questioning process, you may even question your path: a great start to creating change or doubling down on your vision.

Many times, my clients will come to me in the depths of questioning their path, thinking it's a sign of impending doom. It's not. Questioning our paths in life is crucial, and we should be creating enough space on a daily basis for reflection and questioning. That's where powerful initiatives are born.

You feel what peace truly is. When was the last time you felt deep inner peace? For most, the question sounds like a bad joke. Yet, we all want to *feel* inner peace. But it's never been more elusive. We can't spend a moment in silence, let alone not check Instagram for the 87th time today or listen to the latest made-up drama on sports radio or the local news. Inner peace won't be achieved in the day-to-day hustle, it's only going to happen when we disconnect and break the cycle.

Disconnect to reconnect. Disconnecting in life allows for an opportunity to reconnect to what matters. We get caught up in mindless tasks, responsibilities, and a "to do" list that only grows longer every time we knock something off it. For those who run their own businesses, the endless pressure of revenue goals, launching marketing campaigns, and payroll can send us into a tailspin of epic proportions, robbing us of the reason we got started in the first place: freedom.

You remember what's essential. The spiritual leap is a reminder of what's important. By asking the bold and uncomfortable questions, we remember the essential. There are only a few important things in this life. Based on our personal philosophy, we're able to remind ourselves of those and live a more congruent life. That's what we're here for in the first place, *right?*

You're less likely to be reactive. We live in a reactive world. Hopped up on caffeine and noise, we're often running in circles and chasing tails. Okay, that's a nod to Coldplay's brilliant *The Scientist*—but you know what I mean. It becomes impossible to not be reactive. You wake up and, instead of owning your day, it owns you. Your spiritual leap flips the script and propels you to be proactive.

You're more likely to show empathy. Throughout your spiritual leap, empathy will be strengthened—a powerful way to build connection with the world and people around us. Instead of coming from a place of judging others, we can feel what it's like to be in their position. And we can also imagine a place where we are with them, which shifts our entire experience.

You achieve a deeper, clearer connection. A spiritual leap is a deep experience, one designed to strengthen your connection. Your connection with yourself, those around you, your environment, and the world at large. You'll feel more in tune, and the small dramas of life won't seem as big a deal.

Your day-to-day quality of life increases. Last, although some of what I've mentioned is deep and powerful, your spiritual leap is most integrated in your day to day. You know, the way you react to *that* passive-aggressive email, the guy or gal who cuts you off in traffic and flicks you off, or the miscommunication with your spouse about who was supposed to get dinner.

It's within these micro moments that your leap is practiced and cultivated. Instead of seeing something as a challenge in your business, you see the possibility of a solution you never saw before. Instead of getting triggered by your employee's lack of following direction, you can showcase a little empathy when you've been that way, too.

#NotesFromTheLeap

Elizabeth Lyons
Book Publishing Entrepreneur

What's the boldest leap you've ever taken and why was this important to you?

I was driving down the highway and one specific song hit me hard. I'd heard it many, many times before, but I had to pull over. As an irregular crier, I was unable to control the tears that were pouring out of me. My human being wasn't sad; my soul was devastated. I knew it was time to take the leap off the highest cliff I'd ever jumped from. It was time to own who I was, who I wasn't, and who I was ready to step more fully into. That meant a massive shift in every significant area of my life that couldn't be undone once it was done.

What did you feel as you made this leap, and what happened after?

Unbelievably terrified, but it led to freedom, truth, ownership, and peace. It was a "knowing" I was unable to deny. Honestly, I didn't know that it was for me in that I had no idea how it would work out. As a fan of structure and knowing what comes next, it was the scariest decision I've ever made. But the peace I felt in that one instant on the side of the road was enough to carry me through it.

What did you feel as you stared into the abyss and what happened after?

These are the decisions you have to make 100% on your own. You don't ask someone else if it will be okay. You don't ask anyone else what you "should" do. You have to go into the deepest part of yourself and make the decision from that point. And then hold onto that from that point forward through the bumps and roadblock.

I Don't Have Time for This Stuff

In working with high performers who are used to the old model of do more to be more, they're often the *last* to consider a spiritual leap. Why? Well, going to a seven-day meditation retreat doesn't seem to correlate with shattering profit goals. Often, they're deep in the hustle and grind mentality, and have no time to waste. A 37-minute meditation? Come on, Tommy! I've got sales to make, deals to close, and mouths to feed at home. Take your law of attraction crap and shove it you-know-where.

Unless there's a specific output to the input, they place this entire topic under the label of *woo-woo* hacks and one big pyramid scheme where Deepak Chopra is laughing his way to riches.

What you believe is up to you (and it will dictate your results with *any* practice), but what if a spiritual leap led to more *results,* not less? **What if disconnecting from the nonstop noise of the world**

created the necessary space leading to a big business break-through? What if what got you *here*, won't get you *there*? These are the questions I want you to consider if you experience resistance.

One of my clients, Jeff, founded a successful marketing agency. He'd worked for years to build it, and the sweat equity he poured into it was real. And yet, he came to me because he was *stuck* and so was the business. Twenty-three months of record-breaking revenue followed by nine of plateaus. What he thought he needed when he joined the Mastermind group was more business, strategy, and clarity around client acquisition. Except he had tried all that, and it *didn't* work.

What did we start with? Space and a spiritual leap. He committed to 90 days of 15 minutes of meditation, followed by one sensory deprivation (often called floating) session a week, culminating in a three-day intensive meditation excursion.

" ...but Tommy, when are we going to get to the *real* stuff?" he would ask me. I continued to remind him how he came to *me* and sought me out. To his credit, his level of trust in the process was amazing, and he knew a breakthrough would require a new level of thinking.

Without implementing any *new* strategy, the month after his spiritual leap was his best in a year-and-a-half. He shattered the previous months revenue, and then made the key hire he was missing all along: chief financial officer. He was able to increase his salary out of the business by 25%, reduce his personal stress, and find himself re-invigorated with the process. And, oh yeah, his marriage of 11 years was on fire again.

You can choose to believe it was a stroke of luck and a coincidence. Or you can see what happened: *he* shifted, and since he was the heart of the business—that followed suit.

Types of Spiritual Leaps

Spiritual leaps come in *all* shapes and sizes. It's important to remember: it's not about the size of the leap, it's about the alignment and ability to integrate into your life. If you've never meditated, I'd say heading to

Peru for a planet medicine experience *may* be a little much. Although, for the right person at the right time, a radical, immersive leap may be the exact thing they need.

Before we explore the types of spiritual leaps available, I want you to take creative ownership, too. Although I'll outline some common ones with relative examples, feel free to expand and create your own. Remember, taking ownership of your leap is *everything* and will determine the long-term impact it has on your life. And impact is exactly what we're here for.

Spiritual Leap 1: Explore the Unknown

In this place, you're shifting your experience of life by releasing what you've known and embracing something new. If you're feeling the most resistance, this one's for you. Exploring the unknown will open your curiosity and give you enough of a taste to hopefully come back for more and dig deeper.

This can be anything from a half-day meditation experience to committing to the study of a deep spiritual text. This is a starting point to deepen your exploration and begin the process of your quest.

The key with his leap is to get comfortable in the uncomfortable of silence and quiet. If you've been running on fumes and never get a moment, this will nourish and challenge you. This is your starting point of your experience, and the moment you truly embrace the power of the inner quest.

Spiritual Leap 2: Deepen Your Practice

You're already on your path, and you're ready to deepen it. You've experienced some leaps and have practices rituals centered around space and reflection. But you're barely scratching the surface, and you know it. You want more.

The initial leaps only intensified your desire to shift, and it's time for something bold and exciting. This type of leap involves an *experience* in which you break the pattern of your daily life. It could look like a three-, five-, or seven-day retreat or excursion. You've wanted to do this before but gave in to the common excuses of time and responsibilities. Dig in, because you're going deep and will come out a changed person.

Spiritual Leap 3: The Radical Leap

Sometimes in life, we need to rip the Band-Aid off and go *all in*. The radical leap is exactly as it sounds, a complete shift in perspective, and not for the faint of heart. This leap could look like a whole host of options, including: immersive experiences, long retreats, and intense journeys designed to go inward. The key ingredients here are radical disconnection and for your reality to be ripped wide open.

During your radical leap, you will unquestionably come back as a different person, and you know it. You're constantly searching for new ways to grow, and this type of spiritual leap will take you there. You're ready, and you can't wait to experience it.

Spiritual Leap 4: Micro Leaps

Although all types of spiritual leaps have benefits and are a great starting point to get you emotionally anchored to the feeling, you'll also have micro leaps along the way in the form of practices.

Most often, the most transformative benefit you'll experience during your leap won't happen *during it*, it'll happen *after*. This is the integration process when you come back to daily life. Shane Stott, CEO of Float Tank Company, develops cost-effective floating devices for those who want to tune in to a deeper part of themselves, cure past trauma, and find balance in their lives.

Floating, or sensory deprivation is lying in a zero-gravity tank with thousands of pounds of Epsom salt keeping you buoyant. You close the door, you're in total darkness, and you lose the ability to use your senses. In speaking with Shane, he expands:[4]

Just going floating gets your analytical mind out of the way. You feel a sense of peace and calm unlike anything else. And the best part: the biggest benefits come the moment you step outside of the tank.

Think of micro leaps or practices to fuel you between the bigger leaps along your path. Each one acts as a bridge to deepen your experience and share your new gifts with the world.

What's (Always) in the Way

Undoubtedly, there will be some resistance towards taking your spiritual leap. That's normal, and I encourage you to lean in. My clients who resist meditation and rituals of space the most are always the ones who *need* it the most.

Let's examine some of the common roadblocks with your spiritual leap that can easily stop you in your tracks:

Labeling. A common roadblock to taking a spiritual leap is projecting our beliefs by labeling. This is extremely common. From a statement as simple as "that's not for me" to "all those people are crazy," labeling lets you *off* the hook. It lets you to avoid taking the leap and missing out on what's found during the (sometimes) uncomfortable journey inside.

Fear. Tim Ferris was sitting at a 10-day, Vipassana meditation and wanted to quit. His body ached, and the thoughts going through his head would have disturbed Stephen King. He couldn't take it anymore, and his darkest demons were brimming to the surface. He was ready to leave but stayed with it to find a new level of clarity.[5] Most won't take the spiritual leap due to an immense fear of discovering who they really are.

FOMO (fear of missing out.) The fear of missing out will be a common roadblock to taking your leap. Missing out on the rest of life—the logical and rational parts of your identity, including your business, career, your tasks, bills, responsibilities, and the countless roles we play. Stack on breaking news, sports updates, and missing the endless rolodex of social media status updates, and fear of missing out stops us cold. Most of us are addicted, and breaking the addiction proves to be a challenge.

Avoidance. What was she *looking* for? I kept asking myself. I was deep in a spiritual retreat in Sedona, Arizona and I questioned why the hell I even came. We were going through a forceful breathwork experience designed to release emotional build up. I felt resistance, and I didn't want to let go. I remember telling myself: *Dude, can't you be normal and fall in line without always trying to grow?* And that's when I knew I was being overwhelmed by resistance.

Ultimately, I had a life-changing experience where I achieved massive clarity on deep issues such as death, emotional scars, and self-acceptance. But getting there wasn't easy. Going within is a journey of deep exploration and uncomfortable questions. You're going to want to quit. You're going to want to bow out. Stay with it, and let the magic unfold.

Practical Tools for Your Spiritual Leap

Your spiritual leap and practice will have a powerful set of tools, habits, rituals, and practical ways of deepening your experience. There are countless ways to do this, so I'll highlight some favorites and essentials.

Meditation. No need to go deep here, because the research is obvious: meditation is a must-have tool in your arsenal. If you're looking to achieve more inner peace, clarity, and go within, you can't go without this practice. There are countless ways to do it, and all types of formats. Pick one and stick with it. Remember: if you struggle with it, it's because you're human.

Breathwork. One of the greatest tools we have is one we rarely think about, yet we already perform over 23,000 times a day: breathing. This forgotten tool is a gateway to turn stress into peace, and chaos into calm. There are countless types of breathing, which I'll add to the resources section. But don't ignore the power of your breathing, I've had life changing experiences only using intense breathing.

Sensory deprivation. Imagine floating in space. Now you can, thanks to zero-gravity sensory deprivation, or floating. We already discussed floating previously but it simply means being in an isolated capsule full of thousands of pounds of Epsom salt. This is my favorite of all the tools, because you've got nowhere to go, nowhere to be, and nothing to do.

Cold-water therapy. There is *nothing* like stepping into a 40-degree cold tank to find out what you're about. But cold-water therapy isn't limited to the mental benefits; the physical benefits include a powerful release of endorphins designed to make you feel better and fight inflammation at a moment's notice.

Advanced techniques. There are countless techniques designed to help you deepen your spiritual leap and practices. This is not about religion or believing in anything if you don't want to. It's simply about creating space in a hectic world. In this space you'll find powerful insights you won't find anywhere else. Get started, release expectation, and let the advanced practices come to you.

Your Spiritual Leap

If there was *one* leap designed to help you navigate the rest of your life, your spiritual leap is the one. But often, we wait until a challenging crisis occurs to remember what matters. By taking matters into your own hands, you'll be able to move through the seasons of your life with more depth and inner peace.

Furthermore, your connection to others (and to yourself) will improve. You'll rest a little easier at night, knowing you've cultivated a strong connection to something much bigger and bolder than our day-to-day responsibilities.

And best of all, you'd have built a powerful foundation to lean on when you're in need of answers.

Chapter 12 Key Takeaways

- **The most powerful insights happen when there is space.** Stress, anxiety, and an endless to-do list aren't where you will find the deep insights for life and business.

- **Spending time in quiet solitude is crucial to growth.** This works on several levels and is a key marker to how fulfilled you are with yourself, and your life. Be intentional with creating the space and loving it.

- **Our spiritual foundation must be met.** Otherwise, we will feel empty and disconnected. Create a practice or set of rituals designed to deepen this connection daily and quiet the noise from the external world.

CHAPTER 12 LEAP POWER STEP

What is the one decision you've been putting off in your spiritual connection?

_____

_____

What's been holding you back from making this decision and why?

_____

_____

What are you committed to doing now?

_____

_____

Notes

1. https://www.businessinsider.com/twitter-ceo-jack-dorsey-does-vipassana-meditation-2018-1.
2. Email and phone interview, September 2018.
3. Private interview, September 2018.
4. https://resistaverageacademy.com/shanestott/.
5. https://www.goodlifeproject.com/podcast/tim-ferriss-tribe-mentors/.

Chapter 13

The Connection Leap
(Love Out Loud)

Rachel Hollis knew it was time. She'd been married to her husband for 12 years and the future looked bleak. She knew if she continued this path, they were destined for divorce. With four kids, and managing the day to day of her business, she needed to have the conversation. She had been growing personally and professionally, and he'd long been stagnant.

She was scared shitless. So, she put it off, and kept telling herself it would happen when the time was right. Days passed. Weeks passed. And months passed—and still she said nothing. The feelings only grew fiercer every time she didn't listen and avoided what she knew she must do.

Then, she reached her breaking point. Explaining the dire circumstance in her own words: *"I knew if things didn't change, we wouldn't be married in two years. We were growing apart."*[1]

After an especially trying family vacation when her husband spent most of the time disconnected, she couldn't wait any longer. The kids went to bed that night, and she psyched herself up; it was happening, and it was (likely) going to hurt. But she leaned in anyway.

It was messy. It was emotional. But it was the wakeup call they *both* needed. That night, everything changed for them as individuals and as partners. Today, they consider this one conversation to be the breakthrough they needed to get to where they are now: connected, on fire, and thriving. Rachel Hollis shook the world with her book, *Girl, Wash Your Face,* selling over a million copies, launched two podcasts in the top 10 (one with her husband, who quit his corporate gig at Disney and now is CEO of her company) and, most importantly, rekindled the most important part of her life.

I know what you're thinking: how could one conversation be considered a leap? I get it. I'm here to remind you the leaps of our lives don't always come in the ways we'd expect. But the result is the same: a radically different life, and in Rachel's case – saving her marriage, family, and connection because she had the audacity to speak up.

She stepped into the unknown while in the (seemingly) most known place: her closest relationship.

And your connection leap will be similar.

Not All Sunshine and Rainbows

I could have started this part of the connection leap with a feel-good story about someone taking a chance on love, moving cross-country to meet their soul mate, or proposing after only 11 days to live a lifetime of bliss. But this isn't a Hollywood romcom (I do *love them*, though). And although those stories can all be leaps, they don't always happen from a comfortable place.

There is no doubt we tend to grow comfortable in relationships and take them for granted as time passes. Often, this happens as a result of a more pressing pursuit: our careers, the business launch, or simply managing the day to day of life.

And yet, what gets lost is often the most important: our core relationships. Enter the Grant Study, the 80-year (and counting) comprehensive study on what drives happiness and fulfillment. Number one on the list: meaningful relationships. Obvious, right? Not always. Not only were core relationships the most important pillar, they led to success across all other areas of life. The study expands:

> Vallant notes that the 58 men who scored highest on the measurements of "warm relationships" (WR) earned an average of $141,000 a year more during their peak salaries (between ages 55–60) than the 31 men who scored the lowest in WR. The seventy-five years and twenty million dollars expended on the Grant Study points to a straightforward five-word conclusion: Happiness is love. Full stop.

So, not only do our connections provide fulfillment, they make us more profit and bleed into other areas of our lives. I don't know about you, but creating a powerful intimate relationship has been my *best* business breakthrough.

The connection leap is about remembering what matters: those closest to us. Sometimes, it's about letting go or taking a radical chance on love. It can mean facing ultimate rejection and putting every part of your soul on the line. Or it can be about nourishing your closest relationships and re-committing in a bold way.

Who It's For

We've all experienced an incredible connection in our lives, and the flip side—the missed opportunity. A chance encounter, the person we felt deeply connected to, and yet we let our heads win and made excuses about why it *wouldn't* work. Somehow, we talked ourselves out of it.

Relationships are both the place where we experience the beauty of life and where we're pushed to our edge. There's no better place to discover the entire spectrum of what makes you and I who we are. And there no better place to experience love, passion, and a sense of being with the right person at the right time.

So, who is the connection leap for?

If you're ready to take a bold chance on love, this is for you.

If you've been feeling disconnected in your relationship, this is for you.

If you've felt alone and lacking a partner in crime, this is for you.

If you know you're finding yourself in the wrong movie with the wrong person, this is for you.

If you know there's someone out there who's going to light your soul on fire, this is for you.

If you've gotten lost in the day to day of life and forgotten what a deep relationship feels like, this is for you.

If you've neglected your relationship with yourself and looked for others to fill this void only to be disappointed, this is for you.

Waking Up Alone

I was *crushed*. I'd just told my girlfriend of three years the vision deep in my heart, and she wasn't buying it. I'd declared exactly what was going to happen with creating and growing a fitness business of my own, helping people achieve incredible transformation. I was on fire when I said it, and then it all came crashing down as she said to me:

"Yeah, right. That's *never* going to happen."

The truth is, I'd been holding on to something long past the expiration date. I *already* knew this. Yet, like many of us, I was terrified to let go. Instead, the Universe decided to make me let go in an entirely different manner, I'd encouraged her to start a new fitness program, and she cheated on me with her new trainer.

The Universe will always take the wheel when you don't. Yet again, I learned my lesson. When the chaos ended, I woke up alone. And while the pain was real, it was also magical and served as a reminder: before I step into a relationship with someone else, I must step into a powerful relationship with myself. The rejection I felt didn't come from someone else; it came from rejecting myself and seeking to fill the void through someone else.

The next two-and-a-half years, I barely dated. I said no to opportunities and chose to focus on *me*. I wanted to discover myself and, most important, I wanted to figure out what my standard was in a partner and be willing to wait it out until it came to life. Through this process, I learned to love being completely alone, in solitude. I forged a power-couple relationship with the person in the mirror: his flaws, weirdness, and greatness.

This was one of the many connection leaps I've taken over the years. I chose this one to illustrate that sometimes, much like Rachel Hollis, this leap can involve discomfort. But on the other side is a connection you can't imagine. Someone with you on every level: mental, physical, emotional, and spiritual.

Someone who has your back, no matter what. But like anything else in life, it starts with *you*.

Self-Love Is the New Black

Take a moment and reflect on some of the most vital relationships in your life. Start with yourself, and what your connection to you looks and feels like. Think about how you feel spending long periods of time by yourself. Think about what it feels like to look in the mirror:

What do you see? How do you feel? What's missing? Where do you place your focus?

For many, these moments tend to be fleeting. They can't get out fast enough, because we're wired to focus on what isn't working.

You're not fit enough.

You're missing something.

You're not worthy or capable.

Self-love is the new black. All roads lead back to the same place: the level of appreciation you have for yourself. You can make all the cash, you can launch the dream business, you can even have a powerful significant other, and amazing kids. But without self-love, and the ability to look in the mirror and own your greatness, none of it feels *quite* right. I've always said, **without self-love, your failure and success can crumble you equally.**

I get what you're thinking: *you're a guy talking about self-love?* I am, and I'm proud of it: I've had to endure pain, questioning, and tears to get to this place. I don't care if you're a CFO, an eight-figure entrepreneur, mother of three, or a world class athlete, without focusing on yourself, your fulfillment will be held hostage and your results will be fleeting.

Leap Tip: Date Yourself

Every Wednesday afternoon, I have a block of time scheduled out— *"ME TIME."* My clients do, too: a weekly, nonnegotiable date with number one.

Yes, you're going to date yourself. What you do on this date is up to you, and some of my favorites are a massage, a haircut, going to a movie alone, walking in nature, and so on.

You'll not only be reinvigorated, you'll continue to deepen the connection with yourself. Spending time in solitude is magical for your heart and soul.

The Benefits

Your connection leap will be an incredible source of inspiration and will fuel every part of your life. It will keep you grounded when you're lacking clarity. It will demand you become the greatest version of yourself. It'll help you raise your standards.

I could have settled along the way. It wasn't until I *woke up* through a painful break up and cultivated a powerful relationship with myself in which I raised my standards. I decided I wouldn't settle, even if it meant years or a decade to find my match. I'd be so comfortable alone that I didn't need anyone to fill me.

And when the universe provided me a 15-second window of opportunity on a random Tuesday, I was able to step into it fully. I was able to embrace it and take a momentary risk for a lifetime of rewards.

Your connection leap can and will provide you:

- **A deep connection to fuel you.** There is nothing like the feeling of being *connected*. We crave it, and it is hard wired into our hearts and minds to seek it, create and nourish it. On the path of life, a feeling of disconnection leads to chaos and uncertainty.
- **A powerful presence and clarity.** Have you ever experienced an issue in your relationship, been somewhere else and couldn't focus on anything *except* the issue? Yeah, we've all been there. When our relationships are out of alignment, it impacts every area of our lives. We wake up thinking about it and go to sleep the same way – keeping us stuck and clouded.
- **An unmistakable sense of belonging.** We *all* want to belong. We want to be heard, valued and appreciated. Our core relationships provide this sense of worthiness and belonging. Both are crucial to our mindset and emotional stability as we navigate life.
- **Provide an unbreakable foundation.** Our relationships become our safe harbor as we navigate the complexities of our lives. They are a place where we can let our guards down and truly express ourselves. If done right, they provide an unbreakable foundation.

Types of Connection Leaps

There are all types of connection leaps available to you: sometimes with yourself— your most intimate relationship—or taking the lead on organizing the trip with the close friends you haven't seen in years. What matters is the *depth* of the leap, to ensure a radical shift in perspective and meaning. Let's explore some common options available to you.

Connection Leap 1: Turning to You

"I don't know if I can keep going, man. This is hard."

I'm sitting three-quarters of the way into my favorite hike in Phoenix, one I've done 117 times in less than three years. My client flew in from Los Angeles for a one-day intensive hike to create a game plan for every part of his business and life.

But I don't start in a conference room at my office. Instead, we're on the mountain and it's a brisk 103 degrees. It's July. Steve is 44 years old. He made $200,000 in personal income last year. He's got three kids. And he's here with me in the sweltering heat, carrying an enormous rock on his shoulders. It hurts. And oh yeah, he *paid me* to do this.

"You're focusing on the pain, and that's why it hurts. Start identifying what the rock means to you, and why you're carrying it. Let's go, you're playing small."

And the path continues. He grimaces every step of the way. The rock is uncomfortable by design: no matter how one carries it, it restricts breathing. The mountain is hard enough; the rock makes it harsher.

Although I won't reveal every part of this experience, it culminates in a moment at the top when we express gratitude for the rock and the lessons it brought us. The rock, as you may have guessed, represents the baggage you and I carry. It's not only the roadblock to clarity, growth, business production, and so on; it's what's in the way of fully appreciating who we are. We finish with letting go of the rock, and feeling the freedom, joy, and fun of *not* holding on to it anymore. Once this happens, everything is possible.

The first connection leap is about you. What this looks and feels like is up to you: an entire day alone, a trip by yourself, an experience designed to reconnect with the person in the mirror.

Connection Leap 2: The Reconnection

None of us wakes up and declares we want to feel disconnected and a lack of intimacy in our relationships. At least that I know of. And yet, how do we wind up there time and time again? I don't need to tell you the latest stats: relationships are fading faster than ever. The numbers are abysmal.

The second connection leap is about reconnection and pouring back into the most important relationship in your life. It's about recognizing you're responsible for allowing the magic to fade, and you stopped doing the little things: the date nights, the notes of affirmation, the flirting from the early days. Committing to reconnecting in your relationship or marriage can be one of the boldest leaps you can take.

Connection Leap 3: Letting Go (the Release)

We always know. Much like my earlier story about being cheated on, we always know when the expiration date on a relationship has come and gone. And yet, we hold on, using our heads to find the reason to stay. Except, because we know the truth, it doesn't work. Worse off, we wind up resenting ourselves.

Break ups are *hard*. We all have experienced one. But sometimes, the greatest gift we can give ourselves (and someone else) else is moving on. Through this process, we find a deeper part of ourselves we had forgotten and create space for something and someone *new* to come to us.

Clinging to a relationship that isn't for us has countless consequences. First, the emotional rollercoaster it brings us can be devastating. Second, there's the opportunity cost—knowing every day we stay in our current reality, we're missing out on potential chances.

Am I saying to march over to your significant other right now and end it? No. But if you've grown apart, if your paths are going in completely different directions, if you've done everything you can to reconnect, it may be time to let go. However painful, there lies a new possibility on the other side.

Remember: no matter who comes in and out of your life, there will always be one common denominator: you.

Connection Leap 4: Going All In

It's never the right time to go *all in*. Often, we live by societal rules and external pressure for timelines in our relationships. We feel we must do something bold, and yet we sit and wait until the time is right.

The time will never be right until you choose to make it so. Going all in may look like finally proposing to your special someone. It may look like choosing to ditch the long-distance relationship and moving in together. It may be like taking the trip of a lifetime before you feel ready. It may be taking the next bold step.

Last year, during a meditation, I experienced a vision in which I proposed to my now fiancée in my favorite city in the world. The timing didn't make sense, and my head wanted to wait, but that evening, I booked our flights. At the time, I hadn't budgeted for a ring, and business was intense. On the surface, it didn't seem to make sense.

And yet, because of this leap I was able to ask my soul mate to marry me overlooking the beautiful beach of this Basque town in Spain and experienced one of the most incredible days of my life.

Going all in is about taking a chance, doing what you feel called to *now* and making a bold decision on love and connection.

#NotesFromTheLeap

Nick Matiash
Teacher and Men's Life Coach

What's the boldest leap you've ever taken and why was this important to you?

My wife shook up my world. I met her at a time when I was recently single (after 4.5 years of dating my ex), living an hour-and-a-half from her, and wasn't really all that interested in a relationship. Then we went on a couple dates, I fell hard, and moved my life to her, proposed, and now my life's incredible.

What did you feel as you made this leap, and what happened after?

I honestly didn't have a lot of rational reasons to pursue it, it just felt like it was right. Logic didn't make sense, but I was emotionally all in. Excited, nervous, and optimistic all wrapped in one. Now I'm in an incredible marriage, experiencing fatherhood, and in an environment that allowed me to become the man that I am now.

Looking back, what would you tell someone else in a similar circumstance knowing what you now know?

TRUST YOUR GUT! And then the process.

What Gets in the Way

We know what to do yet can't make ourselves follow through. We feel a pull in our hearts, take out a notepad, and talk ourselves out of it. Often, the same patterns and themes get in the way of our connection leap, including:

The ego. Our egos always get in the way of love and connection. Why? Because the ultimate fear of the ego is being exposed and hurt, and it will do anything to protect us. In relationships, it always wants to be *right*. When we want to share something deep and vulnerable, it stops us. During arguments, it doesn't want to show empathy and understand the other side. There is no better place to dissolve the ego and learn to connect than in our relationships.

Our baggage. We *all* have baggage, and we bring this baggage into our relationships. Often, they become someone else's burden. It doesn't matter if you had a picturesque childhood or suffered trauma, we have emotional blocks that keep us from fully stepping into our power in relationships.

Fear of rejection. This fear is constant, and we've all felt what it tastes like to be rejected by someone else: it hurts. So, we can be more guarded and less open in an effort to avoid this feeling once again. But this is missing out. Your connection leap will force you to face rejection head on and carry on anyway.

Complacency. Why do relationships that were once thriving and full of life now seem distant and cold? As we mentioned earlier, complacency is an easy trap to fall into and we forget how special our connection really *is*. We forget to be curious and to recognize the human in front of us for what they are—a miracle. We normalize amazing with the people closest to us and pay a heavy price.

The nonessential. As we step into complacency in relationships, we can lose focus on the what truly matters. In chasing business success, we can forget the small details that provide deep connection with others: date nights, special messages, notes, and even flirting. Your leap will require you to never lose the spark in your connection and remember to put it as a constant priority in life.

Be the Leader with Vulnerability

Dr. Brené Brown, researcher at the University of Houston and best-selling author, is an expert in what creates lasting social connection. During her years of conducting thousands of interviews and studies she found one common bond between the strongest of connections—*vulnerability*.[2]

What exactly is vulnerability? Simple: being open and letting our guards down. I keep it simple: **it's about being human, and letting others *see and feel* our humanness**. And yet, so often we're waiting for someone to give us permission to do so. We wait until others share their truth, and then we do.

Instead, take the lead and put yourself out there in all types of connections. Most people are waiting for someone to be the leader, and they can finally exhale. No, it's not easy; it's not supposed to be. But taking an emotional risk leads to endless rewards in life, career, and business.

When I meet someone for the first time, I never talk about the places I'm on fire with my life. Why? Because I want to connect and share some of the challenges I'm wrestling with. In turn, they do the same. Instead of our conversation being a one-way monologue where we each share our ego-filled highlight reel, we leave empowered. If done right, we both are able to express our challenges (which is naturally therapeutic) and go one level deeper than usual.

Consider vulnerability your secret sauce to create impactful connection with those around you—people who truly have your back and will be there for you no matter what. And for your leap, it's a nonnegotiable ingredient.

Leap Tip: Lean in to Vulnerability

Once a day, practice getting vulnerable. Don't overthink this—it's about telling someone how you feel, when you feel it. It's about sharing a challenge with someone. It's about speaking up during the meeting and sharing what matters to you. It's about connecting with a stranger and letting them see and feel you.

This practice has endless benefits: deep connection, inner peace, and a feeling of freedom.

Put Yourself on the Line

We attempt to put love and connection on timelines. We try to mix logic and reason to make decisions that don't abide by those rules. Often, it leads us to feel alone, disconnected or like something is wrong with us. Worse, it can lead to fragmented relationships with those who matter most.

Instead, flip the script and put yourself out there. Take the chance, what do you have to lose anyway? **Rejection is better than regret, and a *no* simply means there's a bigger and bolder *yes* waiting for you.** Regardless what your connection leap looks like, the way it's going to feel is transformative and unlike anything else. Hold on to this energy and have the courage to do what you know you must do: lean in and go.

And never, ever look back.

Chapter 13 Key Takeaways

- **Connection is life-force energy.** Without deep connection in our lives, we feel alone and lost. It starts with us and then with our closest relationships.

- **Self-love is essential.** Without it, we'll always be trying to fill a void that simply can't be filled without loving ourselves unconditionally. Learn to honor the parts of yourself you tend to hide or shy away from.

(continued)

- **Be the *vulnerability* leader.** Take the emotional risk and allow others around you to follow suit. People will feel they can trust you, which is the key to enduring relationships.

CHAPTER 13 LEAP POWER STEP

What is the *one* decision you've been putting off in your connection and relationships?

_____

_____

_____

_____

What's been holding you back from making this decision and why?

_____

_____

_____

_____

What are you committed to doing now?

_____

_____

_____

_____

Notes

1. https://www.letsrise.co/podcast/.
2. https://www.ted.com/talks/brene_brown_on_vulnerability?language=en.

III

Turning Point: The Leap of Your Life

W e've explored all of the types of leaps available to you during Part III, and you will never be the same. There is a clear before and after, a line drawn not in the sand, but in the *cement*. Embrace this energy, because it will propel you to places you could have never imagined, nor thought were possible for you. It's time to do one thing: leap.

As we close out Part III, it's time to ensure your leap doesn't simply become one exciting experience; it becomes who you are. With this comes a great responsibility: to help others make bold decisions for their lives, which you now have become an example for them to follow.

Complete the following questionnaire before moving on to Part IV as we finish our experience together.

Part III Turning Point: The Leap of Your Life

Out of everything we covered in Part III, what resonated the most?

_____

_____

_____

_____

_____

Why did this specific piece resonate with you? Dig deep.

_____

_____

_____

_____

_____

What area of your life are you committed to taking a leap in, and why?

_____

_____

_____

_____

_____

PART

IV

Coming Home

Furthermore, we have not even to risk the adventure alone; for the heroes of all time have one before us, the labyrinth is fully known; we have only to follow the thread of the hero-path. And where we had thought to find an abomination, we shall find a god; where we had thought to slay another, we shall slay ourselves; where we had thought to travel outward, we shall come to the center of our own existence; where we had thought to be alone, we shall be with all the world.

—*Joseph Campbell*

Chapter 14

Brave New World

A s Lisa Nichols sped down the highway in her 1994 Ford Explorer packed to the brim with everything to her name, she drove 97 miles south. With her five-year-old son in the passenger seat, it hit her: she *did* it. She'd left the known, the comfortable, and all the safety nets of security in exchange for the thrill of possibility. She hadn't accomplished anything yet—except everything in the world; she had taken the *leap of her life.*

"Driving down the highway, there was this immense joy that I had already done it. But that wasn't the I did it called creating my life, but that I gave myself a chance. I trusted myself to give myself opportunity to buy my freedom and I did it. You don't want to leave this place having not given yourself a chance to do the thing."[1]

Facing the unknown, she felt a duality of excitement mixed with fear *of not knowing.* This is the leap in action. You've made the decision. You've had your moment. And now, you've crossed the threshold into a brave new world.

What happens now?

#NotesFromTheLeap

Mike Zeller

Founder, Trim Apparel and Rising Starts Mastermind

What's the boldest leap you've ever taken and why was this important to you?

I've had several, including starting a clothing company, but joining Tony Robbins and his platinum partnership meant investing $100K + in myself.

What did you feel as you made this leap, and what happened after?

I felt both scared, excited, and pumped because I knew I was about to embark on a massive transformation. It created massive income shifts, possibility shifts as I saw a different realm of possibilities than I did before. Some of my wounds from prior relationships were healed as well, as I had just gone through a broken engagement then. I owned myself more as a man.

Looking back, what would you tell someone else in a similar circumstance knowing what you now know?

Do it! You've got one life.

You Will Never Be the Same (Act Like It)

Your life has *radically* changed. It's a beautiful intersection of inspiration mixed with trepidation, and yet you can barely contain the excitement. Life feels full again. Your enthusiasm is off the charts. You chose yourself, and the energy this brings can be felt from a mile away.

You'll never be the same. Now is the time to follow up your leap by fundamentally changing who you are. This means the old you is now gone, and you make choices, decisions, and habits based on who you are today and who you're becoming. This brave new world is yours, and yet you must be reminded. Just because you had the courage to bet on yourself in a bold way, doesn't mean it's over. In fact, I want you to know **you're only getting started.**

In this chapter, we're going to explore how to navigate your brave new world. You're going to learn to deal with the energy of excitement, and make sure it goes in the right places. You'll also learn how to deal with fear, uncertainty, and the vulnerable position coming from radical change. You'll develop a set of habits to make your success rely less on willpower, and more on automatic behavior while asking the *right* questions.

Buckle up, because it's time to ensure your leap is a massive success.

Learn to Love Duality

You've taken the leap, so now you're destined for success, right? Not entirely. Although taking the leap in your life is your *first* step to a living the life of your dreams, it's only a step. I'd be doing you a massive disservice if we didn't explore how to bulletproof your leap from both a mindset level (how you think) and a practical level (specific action steps) to maximize your success.

Early on, you're going to be experiencing highly charged emotional states. This means you're going to have extremely high *highs* and also some deep *lows* and moments of questioning. Don't fret, this is par for the course when you make bold decisions and I'm here to make sure you stay on your path.

The first step is simply getting comfortable living in daily duality. You're going to feel like there's a winner-take-all tug-of-war happening between two paths: excitement and trepidation. Between possibility and questioning. Between passion and uncertainty. And all these are not only entirely okay, but they're also to be expected multiple times a day. Lisa expands during our conversation:

"I feel freedom, and I feel fear. I feel freedom to go create, I feel fear because I'm completely in the unknown. This is where people need to live: in a constant duality, and always leaping in the face of fear."[2]

This is normal. And yet, you're going to have to learn to detach from your emotional state to be a deciding factor on whether you execute today, or don't. Here's the conventional wisdom we're led to believe in regard to this:

When I feel motivated and inspired, *then* I'll execute.
When I feel excited and on fire, *then* I'll act on my dreams.
When I feel powerful and clear, *then* I'll be in the game.

It doesn't work that way. You can't afford to rely on those states for your success. Because no matter how impassioned you may feel today, it will fade. There is a natural ebb and flow to everything we do, but placing our ability to move forward on whether we *feel* charged is a bad idea.

Furthermore, it's reverse thinking. **Although counterintuitive, the way you to continue to create the charge in your life is simple: execute with relentless drive, especially when you *don't* feel like it.** In other words, execution is the precursor to the charged feeling, not the other way around.

Want more motivation? Execute.
Want more confidence? Execute.
Want to quiet the doubts? Execute.
Want to feel confidence? Execute.

Idle time is *not* your friend here and the days of waiting for the feelings to hit you while you're watching *Game of Thrones* are long gone, amigo. It's up to you to manufacture and create these feelings on demand.

And the only way to do so is to rise above the emotions and execute like you've never done before.

Leap Tip: Create the Feeling You're Waiting For

Don't wait until you feel inspired, excited, or on fire to move forward with your leap. Instead, cultivate these feelings by taking action—especially the days you *don't* feel like it.

Every time you do this, you start to rewire the pattern of needing to feel a certain way in order to move your life forward.

Make Your Success as Automatic as You Can

Years ago, I met a pilot in Costa Rica who spent most of her time cruising 35,000 feet in the air from coast to coast. I was deeply curious about what the life of a pilot was like. How does the thrill of flying feel? I couldn't get these answers fast enough. I assumed I'd spend the next few hours ungluing my jaw from the table.

And that's when she told me the truth: flying is *boring*. She spends most of her time doing robotic preflight and postflight checklists, and 95% of her total flying time is spent on autopilot. As much as I was looking to glorify her skills as a pilot, it had very little to do with her and more to do with complex computers doing all the work.

And yet, planes nearly always get to their destination on time, without much conscious thought, skill, and maneuvering from the pilots.

Why? Well, autopilot of course. And you can do the same for your leap. **Put as much of the fate of your success on autopilot, allowing you to focus on bigger and bolder things.**

This is where your daily habits come in: a systemized set of behaviors you do every single day with minimal thinking and decision-making. At this point, you've read countless books and articles on the power of habits, and yet I'm often dumbfounded at how people *still* don't put their success on autopilot. They'll say things like, "It's too simple" and wonder why they can't put it all together. **If you can't execute on the little details, forget about the life-shifting ones.**

Not you, and not anymore. Remember Chapter 5, Know Yourself? It's time to pull that back up and build a core set of habits around your personal philosophy in addition to your leap. I could easily go into the rabbit hole of habits, but for the sake of simplicity, I'll give you the non-negotiable baseline(s) you'll need in order to maximize your leap every single day.

Mind Habit

Sharpen your mind every single morning. During your leap, you will be vulnerable to comparing yourself to others, and you'll have moments where you want to give in. This is when cheap, destructive, information will come find you. Idle time leads to distraction, becoming an endless cycle robbing you of your leap's success.

ACTION: Read 10 pages, and/or listen to a video or audio designed to remind you of possibility.

Body Habit

Our emotions are often stored and stuck in our bodies. Make no mistake: your leap will carry a lot of emotion and having a way to clear the energy through physical movement is of utmost importance. We've all gone into a workout, gym session, or yoga class with a problem, and left with clarity. You're not off the hook just because you don't like exercise.

ACTION: Move your body every single day. Consistency matters more than duration. Find something you *like* doing, or you won't last.

Spirit Habit

Last, the practice of connecting to a deeper part of yourself will tune your compass to start the day. You'll feel more grounded. You'll be less scattered and be able to detach from any challenging circumstance life is providing at the moment.

ACTION: At least 10 minutes of space daily. Meditate, pray, reflect in silence—your choice. Keep it simple, and don't skip a day.

If you're not willing to focus your energy on intentional practices to make your success automatic, it tells the world how serious you *really* are. One of the main reasons why a set of habits in the morning is powerful is simple: you waste less energy and willpower.

Willpower is real, and we all know we're much less likely to make powerful decisions when we're exhausted. Building your foundation of clarity and purpose becomes nonnegotiable as you navigate your brave new world. Now let's transition into daily, nonnegotiable leap activities you're going to be committing to.

Leap Habit 1: Reaffirm Your Vision Daily

Let me know if this sounds familiar: you go to your local personal development or success seminar. You get hopped up on a heavy dose of motivational caffeine, and the EDM (electronic dance music) is playing full tilt. You have an emotional breakthrough and see your vision in 4K HD clarity. It's your time, and the ride home is an interesting mix of inspiration and exhaustion, but you're all in.

You experience the usual post event crash and are relying on every ounce of willpower to get back to the emotional state under the lights. But it's not working. The kids kept you up, the unexpected medical bill came in for $1,700, and you're wiped out. Time passes, and since you haven't acted, you start to feel guilty. Much like the book we start and never finish and leave open on our nightstand, every time we pass by it, we feel a little more resistance.

And then it fades, and the vision is long gone.

I always talk to people who come back on fire from events and I ask them about their breakthrough. They light up like a Christmas tree, **until I ask what their *daily* practice to connect with that breakthrough is.**

And therein lies the issue: the once-powerful vision fades into our current reality and we become overwhelmed. Your first leap habit, then, is simple: reaffirm your vision every single day.

At least, every single day that ends with a *y*. This simple action is designed to get you back to your original state and set your compass for the day. Take at least five minutes to take yourself back to your vision and start your day with clarity.

Leap Habit 2: Take One (Purposeful) Step

Every single day, you're going to take one step toward your vision. That's it—one step today, and one step tomorrow. Sure, one day you may take 100 steps, but the purpose here is to drill down steady action and ensure you're making action part of your daily routine. The key is to identify the simplest step you can take (so as long as it's aligned with your vision) and do it *before* you do anything else.

So, why every single day?

Build conviction. Building this habit will turn your leap into who you are and build a sense of conviction. This is the underlying feeling of knowing it's going to work out for you.

Celebrate wins. One step every day is the bare minimum, yet no matter what happens the rest of the day, you've won. By doing so, you're releasing the pressure most people put on themselves. The more you celebrate your wins, the more wins you get to celebrate.

Create momentum. Momentum isn't something that falls from the heavens, it's created the moment you take the first step. This is the power of micro-goals. They delete what usually gets in the way: all the noise before we get started. It's the warm-up to your amazing seven-mile run, it's the 250 words you wrote that turned into 2,300, it's picking up the book to read 5 pages and 90 minutes going by. Just start.

Harness exponential growth. Taking a step every day leads to incremental growth, but that's barely scratching the surface. The real power comes with enough consistency where it turns into exponential growth. I wrote about this extensively in my previous book, *The 1% Rule*—but the core theme is simple: on a long enough timeline, there's a radical growth curve to those who stay consistent and take at least one step every day.

Level up your self-esteem and confidence. Self-esteem and confidence are cultivated through action. By taking one step, you're stacking layers of both and cementing your belief one day at a time. The biggest killer of belief is lack of action, when paralysis analysis takes over and nothing gets done.

Leap Habit 3: Create Space to Reflect

The third leap habit is being intentional with periods of reflection or empty space. In a nonstop world, this is rare and often avoided. You'll need this space to connect with yourself, reflect on how far you've come, and get the creative juices flowing.

In a hustle and grind world, down time comes at a premium. There's always more to do, and another task in front of us. It's an endless cycle that leads to burnout, frustration, or even guilt. Since you're in this game for the long haul, we need you fresh. Using the rest of the tools in your arsenal, the demands on your mind, body, and spirit will be high.

What does this look like? We've already identified several options during the Spiritual Leap chapter, but small practices throughout your day to create white space are all your need. Make it yours: walking in nature, a yoga class, journaling, meditation, or even closing your eyes for 30 seconds and taking a few deep breaths can shift you.

Leap Habit 4: Cultivate Faith and Trust

Conventional wisdom states we must *have* faith and trust and believe in the lives we want to create *long* before we see them coming true. And while I completely agree with most of this logic, what's missing is not treating faith as something we do or don't have but, rather, something we nourish and grow.

How do you make that happen? You act *as if*—as if your vision has already come true—and make decisions from the state of mind of already accomplishing your wildest dreams. We've covered this a few times now—where your ability to make decisions as your future self brings you closer to who you are today.

Leap Habit 5: Practice Deletion

Remember *The Closet Principle* from Chapter 6? During your leap, it's going to be easy to get distracted. It's going to be easy to be taken off course. In order to stay focused and intentional, you're going to have to practice *deletion* every single day. Deletion is simply creating physical, mental, emotional and spiritual energy in your life.

The best way to do so is to ask yourself a set of questions before you add something to your plate, and then once every week to take inventory:

- Is this [NEW TASK, ROLE, COMMITMENT] bringing me closer to my vision—or farther away?
- Is this [NEW TASK, ROLE, COMMITMENT] absolutely essential or can I find a better option (or none at all)?
- What can I delete out of my life for this coming week to ensure I focus on what really matters and move closer to my vision?

Leap Tip: Stop Saying Yes to Everything

When we say yes to everything and anyone, we say no to ourselves and our dreams. Now that you have clarity and have identified your priorities, fall in love with saying *no*.

The greatest marker I've found to make powerful decisions today includes three questions:

1. If this commitment was three days from now, would I still say yes?
2. If I was making my dream income right now, would I still say yes?
3. Is this a true "HELL, YES!" or am I simply doing it out of obligation and/or approval?

Use these three questions to make better decisions today for your future and create boundaries around your leap.

Without a rock-solid foundation of personal habits and your leap habits, you won't be able to build the confidence and clarity you'll need with you every step of the way. Most important, you'll be inspired not only by possibility but also by the reality coming to life right before your very own eyes. Remember, your habits add up day after day, until one day you wake up and you can't believe what you're seeing.

Ask the (Right) Questions

Questions. As a podcaster and coach, questions are the most important part of my arsenal. Used right, they create the container for possibility and transformation. Used incorrectly a conversation that could have gone somewhere *magical* doesn't. A client who could have had a breakthrough stays stuck.

And in our lives, it's the same deal. To ensure success in this brave new world, you're going to have to ask the right questions every single day. The right questions will shift your state of mind and allow you to focus on what you can control: your mindset, beliefs, and attitude. The way you execute. The way you show up.

For example:

- What is the *one thing* I can accomplish in my business today that, even if all else fails, I'd be able to sleep at night knowing I moved forward?
- What is the one nonnegotiable in my personal life I'm committed to doing today to give me clarity and peace?
- What skill must I work on today for 30 minutes that will continue to set me apart from others in my field?
- What is one thing I can execute today to build my faith, trust, and resilience toward my leap?

The key is to ask the right questions based on what you want. Often, we find ourselves asking questions based on fear, scarcity, and small-minded thinking. We look at the past to find familiar answers, and yet we wonder why we can't breakthrough. The right questions will be a trusted partner to lean on during your leap.

Bulletproof Your Leap

Navigating your post-leap world is about one thing: ensuring you achieve the highest probability of success. But instead of simply using willpower, you're going to use the power of automatic behaviors, environments, and decision-making to bulletproof your leap. You'll also be asking *powerful* questions designed to help get you instantly clear your mind and get back on track, no matter what happens.

Chapter 14 Key Takeaways

- **Cut out the middleman for feeling motivated.** Instead, execute regardless of how you feel now, to reap the rewards of feeling inspired and motivated later.

- **Use the Five Leap Habits to create your success.** These five leap habits are designed to keep you on track, with clarity, focus, and purpose. Insert these into your day and create strict boundaries around them.

- **Use powerful questions to open up possibilities and to remember what matters.** The higher the quality of questions we ask, the bigger and bolder the answers we create. Used wisely, you can become a master of asking yourself the right questions.

CHAPTER 14 LEAP POWER STEP

Using the tools in this chapter, map out how you're going to integrate the personal habit and leap habits into your day-to-day routine. Ensure you have a strategic, intentional plan in which you come *first*.

_____

_____

Notes

1. Private interview, September 2018.
2. Private interview, September 2018.

Chapter 15

The Evolution of You

When I was 21 years old, my sister sent me a book. Not just any book—it was called *The Way of The Superior Man*, by David Deida. I looked at the cover, and the subtitle was *A Spiritual Guide to Mastering the Challenges of Women, Work, and Sexual Desire*. Uh, are you trying to tell me something here, sis? At that point in my life, I knew I wasn't the master at creating powerful relationships. But still, I immediately labeled the book "not for me" and put it in a box and reminded myself to tell my sister *thanks*, but no thanks.

Two years later, I'd gained (some) maturity and opened the book again. I told myself I'd give it a chance and started reading. During those years, I'd put in a lot of energy toward growing myself. Upon re-opening the book, I remember glancing at the first chapter's head-line: There Is No *Completion*. It Will Never End.

WTH?! I felt depressed.

What do you *mean* it will never end? What do you mean I'll never be able to *rest*? Isn't the point of life to work hard, create powerful results—and then relish in those for the time we have left?

I know, I know. I was still immature and didn't know what *I didn't know*. But these were the questions spinning in my head as I spent the next decade plunging myself in the deepest and most intense experiences with one goal: transformation. Whether it was a spiritual quest in the Red Rocks of Sedona, or 35-mile physical crucibles, or hiring my mentor, Dr. John Demartini, I was *all in*.

Today, I wake up and I read the same exact chapter: There Is No Completion. And instead of feeling dejected, or wondering what's the point: I lean in, smile, and embrace it. No completion means you and I are constantly evolving. There's always more to learn. There are more corners to explore, levels to experience, and chapters to write in our life's story. There's plenty of ink left in our pens, and we're far from done. Between those two times I opened the book, not much changed.

Except *everything* did; I learned the beauty of the journey you and I get to experience called life, and why it is never ending is a gift.

You and I will always be evolving, and our leaps allow us to experience life with more depth and get to the next level *faster*. During this chapter, we'll explore why your evolution is something to embrace, and how to integrate your leaps (and the additional micro-leaps) to ensure your long-term and constant growth during the evolution of *you*.

#NotesFromTheLeap

Seth Mattison
Keynote Speaker, Co-Founder, Just Luminate

What's the boldest leap you've ever taken and why was this important to you?

In 2013, it was three months before my wedding day and I had very little in the bank account. I left the company I was working for, the people who'd mentored me, and launched into the marketplace on my own. I had to exercise faith, confidence, and courage that my ideas were transformative enough to stand on their own. I bet on myself completely.

What did you feel as you made this leap, and what happened after?

I knew I had to do it, or else I'd live a life of regret. I was feeling called and compelled to go deeper, and it wasn't a "should," it was an absolute "must." After I made the leap, I still woke up with anxiety, questions, and doubt if I would be able to pull it off. But I never questioned whether it was the right decision. The boats were burned, there was no going back. I knew the world needed this.

Looking back, what would you tell someone else in a similar circumstance knowing what you now know?

Do the inner work to allow the bigger forces at play to guide you so your decision isn't about external forces. Combine this with the outer work to ensure the world needs what you have to offer, then step into a place of certainty, and go all in.

The Oasis Is a Myth (but Life Is Still Amazing)

The oasis. A far-off land in the future, painted by hand. The sun comes in at the perfect angle, sun-soaked in bliss. This is the future where you've *made* it. The red carpet has been rolled out for you, and there's nothing else you have to do. You get to bask in all the glory of *arriving* and never have to put up with life's challenges anymore.

Okay, you get it. I know if you're here, you don't (fully) buy into this illusion, but it's still seductive. We often believe this, even if it's not conscious. Beneath the surface, we're subconsciously operating under the illusion of the oasis and that someday it will all be over.

It's not true, and we know it. But neither is Santa Claus or the Earth being flat, but for some reason, some still believe. Often, the peak of your mountain will seem oddly anticlimactic, unless you're winning a Super Bowl. But even then, it can seem that way. I know a few people who've reached the pinnacle of accomplishment, and it wasn't what they expected.

Initially, this may seem disempowering. It's *not.* Life is still amazing even without reaching the imaginary oasis. You look at your bank accounts, and they're fuller than you ever thought possible. Your monthly income used to be your *yearly* income. You live in the home of your dreams. You have a deeply connected, thriving relationship. You're as excited about a random Tuesday as you are about the trip to Rome. Most importantly, you wake up and you're *excited* about the day.

This happens, because you were willing to take the leap. And releasing the illusion of the oasis makes you more powerful, not less, because the oasis gets *boring* after a while. I don't know about you, but on the eighth straight day of having (skinny, don't make fun) margaritas on the beach, I'm ready to move on. There's only so much staring at palm trees we can all take. I'm ready to create, to engage in purposeful work, and do things that *matter*. And if you do it right, you'll be as excited to come back to your work and life, too.

Breakthrough Isn't the End, It's the Start

Your leap is a personal breakthrough with ripple effects that will impact every part of your life. It will radically transform you. And yet, breakthrough moments, insight, and those "aha" levels of insight and clarity aren't the *end*.

They're the start. One of the trends I've witnessed in a personal development, success, entrepreneurship world is an obsession with breakthrough, but not with *integration*. **Integration is where the magic happens, where you take a riveting life experience and bring it from the clouds to the dirt.**

The dirt, of course, is our everyday lives. It's standing in the grocery store in a line that hasn't moved in nine minutes and keeping calm. It's receiving the passive-aggressive email, and not listening to the voices to send back an *ALL CAPS*, rage-soaked email. If breakthrough is the Hollywood action movie, integration is filming that movie.

If you've never experienced a film set, it's *boring*. Take your favorite action flick, and it may seem like shooting it is a daily adventure of awesomeness until you realize it's very mundane, and the same exact take has been done 19 times. And it *still* doesn't work. The average Hollywood movie takes 106 days to shoot, and averages 120 minutes of screen time. Simple math says on average, that's 76,320 minutes of film time.

This analogy is designed to ensure you're integrating your break-throughs and not missing out on the gold each one brings to your life. Your personal evolution will have endless breakthroughs, and once you've taken your leap, you'll experience them regularly.

Early on, during my time working with clients, they experience *big* breakthroughs. As time passes, the breakthroughs become less and less common. One day, a client came to me concerned:

"Tommy...I feel like it's been a *while* since I've had a break-through. I don't know what I'm doing wrong, or what we've been missing."

I smiled and reminded him of the following: he'd grown tremendously. I gave him the example of say, a pro basketball player. When they're in high school, they're constantly experiencing breakthroughs. In college, they are less common as they grow and develop their skills. On the NBA circuit, they're the rarest—a couple of times a season, yet the most impactful. The lesson is simple: as you deepen your evolution and growth, you're going to have *fewer* breakthroughs. This is what we want. We will have more time in between, and yet when they do come, **they'll be much more powerful than what you've experienced before.**

Same goes for you.

Always Sit in the Front of the Class of Life (Leaders Are Learners)

All the cool kids sit in the back, right? Not here. If life is our classroom, we get to sit in front of the class every day and glean from its incredible lessons. We open our eyes and dig deep into the countless lessons life sends our way every single day.

Without a doubt, the number-one obstacle in the way of people's long-term growth is their egos. Especially once they've experienced some type of success, egos begin to build forts and block people from advanced growth. It's easy to drop your ego when nothing's working and you're in a crisis. But are you willing to drop it when you've experienced success, in order to reach a new level? The ego is responsible for:

- Thinking you have all the answers.
- Wanting to be *right*—always.
- Putting others down.
- Limiting your growth.
- Getting in the way of executing.

I'm often asked how I'm able to come up with so much content on a daily and weekly basis, including two podcasts per week, two to three social posts with writing every day, two to three long-form blog posts every week, videos, audio recordings, emails, and more. I know, if you follow me, be careful. I always give people a disclaimer: you're going to hear from me a lot.

But here's why: I've adopted a 360-degree model of learning in life. That means, I can receive a powerful download on a morning hike, bringing me a lesson I use that very same day in business. Or, I can hear a conversation at a random Starbucks, gain an insight—and use it on date night to strengthen my relationship.

In other words, we don't have to *wait* until we're in a classroom or seminar setting to experience powerful lessons. If we take the approach of the student, then **life is always offering up lessons to help guide us,** to help take us a *little* deeper. Often, they're the small things that can shift our entire day.

The 360-degree model of learning is available to you every single day, too. In order to make it work, here's what's involved:

1. **Awareness.** Remember, every experience in life is a chance to learn. Start with being *aware* and open to lessons everywhere you go.
2. **Identification.** Something *happened*—an action, an experience, a result. Identify what it was.

3. **Extraction.** What did you learn through the experience or action? Ensure you take a broad approach and package a lesson you could teach someone else.
4. **Teaching.** Last, teach or declare what you've learned. Tell someone about your experience, do a video on social media, or simply declare it through a journal to yourself.

Here's an example of the model: you get an email you weren't expecting, and it riles you up. The tone is passive-aggressive. You shoot back, and for a moment, it feels good to be right. A few hours pass, and you've had time to reflect. Now, you're starting to regret it. You avoid checking your email because you don't want to remind yourself.

1. **Awareness.** Simply acknowledge the circumstance and be honest with yourself.
2. **Identification.** Identify the email encounter and shooting back a response quickly is the experience.
3. **Extraction.** There would be several lessons, but let's choose one: when emotionally charged, creating time to reflect before being reactive is crucial.
4. **Teaching.** The preceding lesson can now be taught in many areas of life and has deepened your perspective.

This model is how you're able to always be learning, growing, and deepening your experience. You don't need to wait until you're at the seminar; you already have a front seat in the greatest classroom out there.

The Beautiful Dance

During your evolution, you're going to be in a constant tightrope, or dance. This paradox is the acknowledgment of gratitude of where you find yourself today *while* seeking a compelling vision.

Even once you've taken your leap, you'll evolve, grow, and be faced with another decision into the unknown. Don't worry; because of your experience and courage, it does get easier with time. You'll start feeling excited as the unknown approaches. You'll feel grounded and ready when you make a new bold decision. You'd have developed a powerful level of self-trust.

Often, I'll work with people who find themselves stuck in the middle of appreciating where they are today, while they look into the seas of the compelling future. They have trouble navigating these worlds, and they believe they have to pick one thing or another. It's not true; the beautiful dance is as it sounds; you'll be living in both. Some push, some pull. There are moments of tension and moments of flow. Just like Lisa's example: duality is a part of life, and we must embrace it.

What's the practical approach to this? Stop setting goals for an entire year, and instead use the 90-day model.

One Year's Worth of Results in 90 Days

We often associate our personal evolution with *big* life events: moving to a new state, launching the new business, getting married, and so on. In goal setting, the conventional wisdom states to set one-year goals, and yet the system is flawed. One year, for you and me is *way* too far away. Besides, it diminishes how much we're able to grow in that time and we tend to play small.

The truth is, you and I are changing every *day*. Physically, mentally, emotionally and spiritually, we are never stagnant. You are not who you were six years ago. That's obvious, right? But less obvious is you aren't who you were three months ago, or even three weeks ago. We are in a persistent state of change, and we must create goals with this model in mind.

Enter the 90-day model, where your intention is to create one year's worth of results in 90 days. Here's the truth: if you absolutely *had* to do it, you would. And nature's universal law of the Pareto principle states time will fill a void. In other words, if you set a goal with one year to do it, it'll take you a year. Take that same goal and compress it in 90 days, and you'll make it happen. Peter Thiel, entrepreneur, co-founder of Pay-Pal and serial investor, takes this to the extreme by asking:

"How can you achieve your 10-year plan in the next 6 months?"[1] The same principle he's promoting is the one you'll need along the way. Note: this isn't about working *harder* but working smarter. Deleting the bullshit, the idle time, the nonessential. It's about creating urgency and deadlines with 90-day targets, knowing if we do it right our lives can look radically different, and from that place, we can create new outcomes.

For example, in writing this book, I could have requested one year of time from my publisher. Anyone who's ever written a book knows it's intense and consumes your every waking moment. And yet, would all that extra time make things better, and would the quality of work increase?

I don't believe so, and in most cases, time makes things worse. With an abundance of time, we are more likely to distract ourselves. We're most likely to think too far ahead and get overwhelmed. We're more likely to compare ourselves to someone else. And we're much more likely to listen to the inner critic.

In order to maximize your leap and accelerate the process, you're going to set 90-day targets instead of yearly ones. **This proximity leaves you *no option* but to dig in and do the work today**. The beauty of the 90-day approach is simple: every day matters. And when every day matters, we tend to focus on the high priority work and not the stuff we talk ourselves into thinking they matter.

Here are the steps to set your 90-day targets:

1. **Pick your "one" thing.** With your leap, and vision in mind, pick one thing that, if it happened, you'd be thrilled and know your dreams are coming true.
2. **Set the outcome goal, and three process goals.** For your one thing, you're going to pick two to three nonnegotiable processes to bring it to life.

3. **Reverse engineer your first four weeks.** With the first two steps complete, you're going to map out the key action steps for your first four weeks. These are the significant actions that aren't always urgent, but deeply important.

4. **Fill your time.** When we fill our time with high priority actions, we don't have space left for the mindless stuff. Block out the time during your week to focus on the preceding steps. No one can interrupt you, and you're unavailable.

5. **Identify your daily action.** To finish off, you're going to identify the daily, non-negotiable action you're committed to. This allows you to focus on what matters and discard the rest.

Done right, you too can experience one year's worth of results in 90 days. This isn't simply a marketing slogan; I've seen it firsthand. The amount of momentum you can create will supercharge your leap. Combining clarity, simplicity, and what truly matters, you'll look back after 90 days and be amazed. The revenue target was hit. The new hire was made. The platform was launched. The side hustle was born. The career shift happened. The book was written. The project came to life.

In other words, everything you could have put off another day, week, month, or year became the priority and you pulled the trigger.

"You've Changed."

"You've *changed*."

An old friend had contacted me as our schedules aligned, and I was in my hometown for a few days. I hadn't seen him in years, and we'd been very close growing up and past college.

Part of me was resisting the entire deal, but I made it happen anyway. Good old nostalgia was pulling me in, but I committed, and I went in with the intention of connecting.

I'm taking the next bite out of my taco, and that's when he stopped me mid-sentence:

"Dude...are you on something? Like some type of drug?" he asked. Silence came upon us, and I was utterly confused.

"Uh...what? I'm excited, man. But the answer is yes: I'm high on life."

The rest of the conversation was awkward, we finished it off and said our peace. The reason he asked that question was because I'd just gone on an enthusiastic rant about life, business, and the pursuit of it all.

And that's when it hit me: we both changed. Not that my change was better than his, or vice versa; these are our unique lives and our paths. Often, we have trouble identifying the change we're creating every single day, because it's so close to us and most things seem to stay the same, until we experience what I did.

When you live boldly, step into your power, and play full tilt, people who were once in your life, are going to leave. You may simply be on different paths. That's okay. But often, when you grow powerfully, you will make other people uncomfortable. They will see you striving to live your best life. They will feel threatened. They're threatened your relationship dynamic will change, or they'll lose you. They feel triggered by your growth as a reflection of what they haven't done. And much like animals, when people feel threatened, they attack.

Whether it's a passive-aggressive comment, making fun of your pursuits, or telling you why it's never going to work out matters little. What matters is you don't play down to their level, or worse; you don't listen to them, and end up playing small.

Each time I've grown, old relationships have faded only to be replaced by those with deeper alignment. People have snickered and made comments that could have brought me down. But here's what I realized, and you will too: **deep down, the people who try to bring you down are secretly inspired by what you're creating.** No, they may never admit it, but we all want to be better. This is a core human driver, and when we see someone else do it, it gives us hope. Even if that hope is masqueraded in fear and criticism, people still feel it. And once the high of attacking someone else has faded and they see you continuing to live your best life, they may choose to shift too.

This is not about cutting people out of your life ruthlessly. **It's about understanding we have people in our lives for a reason, a season, or a lifetime.** A reason could be a co-worker; the reason our relationship exists is purely work driven. A season is someone who is part of our lives when we live in proximity, but when we move away the relationship fizzles. Lastly, we have people who are there for a lifetime: our family, intimate relationships, and those who are meant to be with us until our last days.

By taking your leap, you become the beacon. Others will see your courage and be inspired—sometimes secretly. Others will judge you and do anything to bring you down. This is what you signed up for, and remember, it's not about you. The greatest tragedy of transformation is letting one or two people bring us down. And if we've solidified our vision and purpose, there's no chance in hell a few people can bring us down.

Next time someone tells you you've changed, all you have to say is: "I know. Thank you so much for recognizing it."

Find Your People

Your tribe is waiting. No matter how out of touch you feel with the people around you, there is an entire tribe of those willing to do *anything* to support your leap and dreams. But they won't discover you at Starbucks; you must find them.

There is no such thing as self-made. Behind every "self-made" success is an endless list of a supporting cast, mentors, relationships, and a tribe who was there. They were there when things didn't seem to work. They were there when doubt crept in. They were there when you wanted to give up.

Right now, your tribe is waiting. Earlier we mentioned the tribe you're serving, but this is different; this is your crew. And in order to fully thrive in this brave new world, you'll need to find your people.

But how?

Simple! You go to the places where they're hanging out. You get uncomfortable and put yourself in rooms where you feel like you may not belong. You find unique ways to truly *connect* and deliver value before asking for anything. In other words, you care enough to go just a little above and beyond.

Those around you will determine your long-term success. They become your backbone, and you trust them in great times, and bad. They provide meaningful and potentially life-changing feedback. They challenge you to think and dream bigger. They are your partners in crime on your path to make your dreams come true.

Now let's deep dive into *how* you're going to do this.

Step 1: Find them. You won't find your crew on the couch. You *must* insert yourself in the places where they hang out—coffee shops, co-working spaces, events, activities and environments where they're likely to be. In person always beats virtual, but use both when starting out and go *all in*.

Step 2: Start with one. When looking to level up the people around you, it can feel daunting. Don't let it; and instead pick one person. Each person will be a brick, and one by one you'll start creating a powerful foundation.

Step 3: Deliver value and be different. Next, it's up to you to deliver value and be different. What this looks like is up to you but go out of your way in an (authentic) way to show them you care. You can *always* help someone, no matter how big they are. What's crucial is you take the time and energy to understand how you can help.

Step 4: Play the long game. Often, people try to do the these things within a span of three days and then label the person when it doesn't work. Remember: people are busy and dealing with their own issues. Relationships won't work playing the short game, since everyone can feel this from a mile away. Start small, simple and detach from any outcome. Each time you insert someone new into your circle, there's a *little* less space for those on the fringes.

Do this long enough, and you'll wake up one day with a badass tribe who will go out of their way to open doors you could have never done alone.

What Not to Do (and What to Do)

There are ways to grab people's attention in a powerful way as well as easy ways to get ignored. It's up to your intent, care, and delivery.

Here's what not to say:

Hey, do you have some time to connect?
I'd love to pick your brain sometime. What works for you?
I would love to grab coffee. Can you do next Tuesday?

Facepalm. People will avoid this at all costs, and no one wants their brain picked. Instead, use something like this:

Hey [NAME]: I love your work, specifically (insert something short that represents you dug deep into them, above and beyond what most people do).
I noticed you (insert a problem or issue you've noticed) and I thought this may be of value to you: (insert solution).
Anyway, I know you're busy, so I wanted to keep this brief.
Rock on,
Tommy
P.S. I know it's the least I could do, but I left you a review (or comment, share, attach screenshot).

Before sending any communication, ensure that:

- It doesn't make them do more work.
- You're not asking for anything in return.
- You detach from any expectation of receiving anything.
- You get to the point quickly (this is hard for me, too).

I've used the this tactic to connect with extremely influential people, and it works. Why? Because it's not a 19-page thesis on why they should give you their time and attention. Instead, it's straight to the point *without* asking anything in return.

You, Inc.

Your evolution will be a fingerprint-specific process no one has ever experienced, so enjoy the ride. Furthermore, remind yourself of the courage you've shown by being here and committing to yourself, and your life. On your path, many will be inspired, and some will look to bring you down. It's part of the game called life. Don't forget to acknowledge your growth along the way and remember there are people you will inspire that you'll never know about.

Keep going, and don't ever quit.

Chapter 15 Key Takeaways

- **Breakthrough is the start, not the end.** What happens next is everything: the way you integrate the breakthrough and start living it every single day. Let it become who you are.
- **Leaders are learners.** Take a seat in the front of the classroom of life and be willing to drop the ego, especially once you're experiencing results.
- **Find (or create) your tribe.** Rolling solo isn't a plan for success. No one is self-made; go out and find your tribe to support your leap.

CHAPTER 15 LEAP POWER STEP

On a scale of 1–5 (5 being highest), how supportive is your current tribe for your leap?

_____

_____

If less than a 5, what is one relationship that is no longer serving who you're becoming?

_____

_____

_____

_____

_____

_____

Where does your tribe hang out? Where are they, and where can you find them now?

_____

_____

_____

_____

_____

_____

Notes

1. https://observer.com/2016/07/this-is-how-you-train-your-brain-to-get-what-you-really-want-2/

Chapter 16

Your Declaration

What a *ride*. We've taken an adventure together, and you're one of the few who has come all the way to the end. We've explored the unknown, we've wrestled with how to know you're ready, the shapes and sizes of leaps available to you, and how to use this energy wisely for every area of your growth.

And yet, we're not done, because now it's time to cement your experience and set off to sail. Carrying your core ingredients and toolkit, you'll set off on a voyage of a lifetime: full of thrill, zest, and the most beautiful elixir in the world of a live well lived.

On your terms. On your timeline. On your deepest desires.

Your leap is waiting for you, and it's knocking at your door. And as we come to the end of our experience, it's time to take the first step and declare the *leap of your life*.

Otherwise, it will slowly eat away at you moment by moment. Everything we covered will become a fantasy, *your* fantasy, another video game and could-have-been.

But the world will miss out, and so will you.

The Time Is Now

"Where are you? Here
What time is it? Now
What are you? This moment."

—Way of the Peaceful Warrior, *by Dan Millman*

No more waiting.

No more hoping.

No more wishing.

Just like we started off, you came here because there's a leap in your life that's been calling you. Maybe when we started you didn't know exactly what it was, and now you do. Maybe you knew all along. Likely, you found yourself with a little of both, and now you have clarity. Regardless, the time is now—right here, right now.

Millions of dreams have been lost waiting for the perfect time. You know, the seductive voice in our heads that says:

Once life slows down a little.

When the kids get a few years older.

After you get the bonus from work.

And yet, what we don't realize is that each moment we stay in the same place, we get a little more anchored than yesterday.

This anchor holds us in place, but also becomes a weight to bear every single day. We wear this weight in our glare, in our eyes, and with a voice of painful regret. But we can also slice through it all in one instance **by making a bold declaration of commitment with our leap and never looking back.**

Within that place is a life you can't quite yet imagine.

June 11, 2018, San Sebastian, Spain, 10:09 a.m.

I wake up, and I can feel the last toast of Spanish cava and *one too many* tapas from the evening prior. And yet, it doesn't matter, because I'm next to my soulmate in my favorite city in the world. I feel alive. We look at each other, and without saying a word, tears start coming down our faces.

This is the moment we've dreamed of, the one I felt but couldn't *see* back on that frigid New York evening years ago. Taking a moment to soak it in, I realize: I *did* it. I didn't know how, and yet I still was willing to take the step into the unknown. The leap has changed me forever, and nothing will ever be the same.

Every area of my life is radically different. Most importantly, the person I am is *changed*, and he now believes. He believes in himself. That he is worthy and capable. This is what he's been looking for.

The tears are flowing because this is a moment of culmination: a dream has come true, and whatever was dreamed up on that New York night now pales in comparison to reality. The leap of my life has happened, followed up by micro leaps to create a life I truly can't wait to wake up for.

I share this to help you understand this is available to you, too. Whatever your personal version is, it's ready. It's waiting. But remember: **it won't wait forever, and doors will close**.

The haunting truth is that moment may easily not exist. It could have easily stayed a dream on that 13-degree night. A glimpse of hope. A moment of clarity. A powerful download.

And then nothing, fading into the oblivion.

Over the past four years, I've taken more leaps than I ever have, and I've never felt so inspired and alive. But enough about me, I've been able to facilitate countless leaps for people who knew it was *time*. And while creating a dream life is powerful enough, it pales in comparison to see others give themselves permission to do the same. There is no greater fulfillment than hearing the stories of those who did *it*.

During this time, I've witnessed countless leaps firsthand, including:

- The burned-out corporate executive who launched his own business, tripled his personal income, and never looked back.
- The mother of three who took her passion and was able to create a six-figure income working from home.

- The entrepreneur who was stuck in revenue making the key hire to exponentially grow his or her business.
- The millennial who felt stuck in her environment and moved across the country to find her people.
- The 37-year-old who'd never completed a physical challenge reaching the summit of Mt. Rainier.
- The overworked and disconnected entrepreneur who found peace and clarity during an intense spiritual quest.
- The family of four who ditched the traditional route and rented the RV to travel around the country for three years.

The list goes on and on, but you get the point. And although I identified the *leap*, I don't expand on the endless benefits the leap provided them. The lives shifted. The relationships enriched. The people around them who were inspired to do the same.

And knowing they were destined to get to the end of their days with nothing but a smile, knowing they did what they had to do when it was time.

A life without regrets, wishes unfulfilled, and songs unsung.

Your Declaration

Toward the end of writing this, I was hiking one of my favorite mountains in Phoenix with my friend Seth, and he asked me a simple question:

"Why are you writing this book, and why *now?*" As a podcaster and coach, I appreciate a great question. And of course, I've asked this very same question countless times of myself. You don't write 250-plus pages by chance. You don't endure a creative process simply because it's cool or fun. There's a deep rooted *why*, or else you simply don't finish. Much like anything else, we only endure when we have a reason that matters to us.

And what I said was simple: I can't *not* write it. Because I know there is at least one person out there who needs to get their hands on this. They need to hear this message and give themselves permission.

Or else they may live their entire lives doing everything except the *one* thing they know they must. This is the book I wish I could have leaned on during the moments of doubt before, during, and after my leaps.

But unlike most books, the primary mission of this one was to be different. I didn't write this to be another book that sits on your shelf. I didn't want you to get inspired about your leap and then get lost in the noise of life. I didn't want this to simply motivate you, because there's a lot more effective YouTube content out there to get you riled up.

I wanted to challenge you, because I respect you. **I know there's greatness inside of you, and the path to unleashing it on the world is through your leap**. And now that we're on the tail end of our journey, it's time.

Much like Felix Baumgartner's moments between detaching from the space capsule he took to the edge of Earth's atmosphere and the moment he leaped, this is the time where the magic happens. It's the riveting in-between where every part of you comes alive.

As Felix disconnected his attachments, he realized this was *it*.

There is no turning back. There is no Plan B. There is no safe harbor.

The Leap of Your Life

This book doesn't end with a finely tuned, perfectly edited conclusion giving you a tightly wrapped summary of what we've been through.

Instead, it ends with a commitment. To this point, I've done most of the talking; now, it's your turn. This is your launch pad, and there is nothing else you need for your journey. Your bags are packed, and there's only one thing left to do.

There's no chance you would have made it through if you didn't have something deep within you that needed to come out. Honor it, acknowledge it, embrace it. And then light it on fire.

It's *your* time.

Below, you're going to identify **The Leap of *Your* Life**. I've shared stories, examples, research, and countless themes and patterns of interviewing the world's best, my own experience, #NotesFromTheLeap, and more. All of these were done with one mission, and one mission only: to help you dig deep and extract your leap, so you could get to this place: your declaration.

This is the moment you place your chips in the middle of the table and go *all in*. Declaring your leap is putting yourself on the line. It's having the audacity to trust in yourself and choose yourself.

Here's exactly what's going to happen next:

The Leap of Your Life Declaration

To download your own Leap of Your Life Declaration form, head over to LeapOfYourLife.com.

1. **You're going to identify The Leap of Your Life.**
   The leap of my life is:

   _____

   _____

2. **You're going to declare The Leap of Your Life.**
   This is how I will declare my leap:

   _____

   _____

3. **You're going to go on social media and declare the leap you're committed to—using the hashtag #LeapOfMyLife.**
   This is where I shared my declaration:

   _____

   _____

4. **Then, you're going to pay it forward and encourage someone you know to take the leap of their life and push them to do so.**
   This is who I'm encouraging to take the leap:

   _____

   _____

The Pen Is Full of Ink, Now Go Write Your Story

What you just wrote and declared is your magic. Own it and feel it like you've never felt anything before. Our time is coming to an end, but you're only getting started. With the leap of your life in your hand, you've stepped into your commitment with a bold declaration. Now, you've got a full set of ink with your blank canvas, and it's time to write your story one day, one page, and one sentence at a time.

The world is waiting for you. Your tribe is waiting for you. Strangers whose lives you will impact are waiting for you. Your closest relationships are waiting for you. But most importantly, guess who won't be waiting for you anymore?

You won't.

This shift alone will make the leap of your life the greatest story ever told, and I can't wait to read it.

Carry on, now. I'll see you on the other side.

Chapter 16 Key Takeaways

- "Someday" is no longer an option. It's time to say goodbye to this mindset and make your someday … right now. Trade in all of your somedays for today.
- It's time to declare your leap. There is no more waiting and it's up to you to write the inspiring story of your life.
- Go write your story. Your leap will become an inspiring story unlike any other. Honor this, double down and never, ever look back. It's your time.

Resources

General Resources

- The Leap of Your Life: official resources, downloads, and free guides to help you maximize your leap. http://www.leapofyourlife.com
- Resist Average Academy Podcast: immersive conversations with the world's most sought after thought leaders, experts and entrepreneurs. iTunes, Stitcher, Spotify, Google Play, and where podcasts are found. http://www.resistaverageacademy.com

Chapter 1

- John Tierney, "24 Miles, 4 Minutes and 834 M.P.H., All in One Jump," *New York Times*. https://www.nytimes.com/2012/10/15/us/felix-baumgartner-skydiving.html
- Lisa Nichols, Motivating the Masses. https://www.motivatingthemasses.com/
- Lisa Nichols, Inside Quest Interview. https://www.youtube.com/watch?v=VS5FqBZWpYo

Chapter 2

- Susan Jeffers, Fear the Feel and Do It Anyway. http://www.susanjeffers.com/home/detailtemplate.cfm?catID=2234

- Elizabeth Gilbert, TED 2009: Your Elusive Creative Genius. https://www.ted.com/talks/elizabeth_gilbert_on_genius?language=en
- David Foster Wallace, *Infinite Jest.* https://www.amazon.com/Infinite-Jest-David-Foster-Wallace/dp/0316066524

Chapter 3

- "TIFU My Whole Life. My Regrets as a 46-Year-Old, and Advice to Others at a Crossroad." Reddit post by John Jerryson. https://www.reddit.com/r/tifu/comments/2livoo/tifu_my_whole_life_my_regrets_as_a_46_year_old/
- Lifehack: Painful Regrets Are Necessary Because That's How We Learn. https://www.lifehack.org/508449/painful-regrets-are-necessary-because-thats-how-learn
- Bronnie Ware: Regrets of the Dying. https://bronnieware.com/blog/regrets-of-the-dying/
- NPR: Why We Can't Shake Life's "Coulda, Woulda, Shoulda" Moments.https://www.npr.org/templates/transcript/transcript.php?storyId=550260750
- The Ideal Road Not Taken: The self-discrepancies involved in people's most enduring regrets. http://psycnet.apa.org/record/2017–21180–001
- Embrace your regrets and move forward, psychologist says. https://news.illinois.edu/view/6367/207410

Chapter 4

- Giordano Bruno, On the Infinite Universe and Worlds. www.faculty.umb.edu/gary_zabel/Courses/Parallel%20Universes/Texts/On%20the%20Infinite%20Universe%20and%20Worlds.htm
- 15 Things You Might Not Know About *The Alchemist.* http://mentalfloss.com/article/63535/15-things-you-might-not-know-about-alchemist

Chapter 5

- Living in Alignment with Your Personal Philosophy. https://findingmastery.net/living-in-alignment-with-your-personal-philosophy/

- Dr. Michael Gervais: Finding Mastery Podcast. https://findingmastery. net/category/podcasts/

Chapter 6

- Karan Baraj Online: http://www.karanbajaj.com/
- Understanding the Pareto Principle (The 80/20 Rule) https:// betterexplained.com/articles/understanding-the-pareto-principle-the-8020-rule/
- Marie Kondo: https://konmari.com/
- BJ Fogg, PHD: https://www.bjfogg.com/
- A Different Environment May Break Habits: https://www.apa.org/ monitor/jun05/habits.aspx
- Resist Average Academy Blog: https://resistaverageacademy.com/ leap-of-your-life-spiritual-leap/

Chapter 7

- Seth Godin, Linchpin: https://www.amazon.com/Linchpin-Are-Indispensable-Seth-Godin/dp/1591844096
- Josh Kaufman, The First 20 Hours: How to Learn Anything, TED Talk: https://www.youtube.com/watch?v=5MgBikgcWnY
- Cal Newport: http://calnewport.com/books/so-good/ http:// calnewport.com/books/so-good/
- How to Tell People What You Do in 3 Easy Steps. http://buildingastorybrand.com/minisode-1/
- Donald Miller, Story Brand: https://buildingastorybrand.com/

Chapter 8

- Tyler Perry, *Higher Is Waiting*. www.penguinrandomhouse.com/ books/534121/higher-is-waiting-by-tyler-perry/9780812989342/
- Tyler Perry, A Place Where Even Dreams Believe. https://www .youtube.com/watch?v=ydqTZqoN0Qk
- Take a Tour of Tyler Perry's Massive New Studio on a Former Army Base in Atlanta: http://www.latimes.com/entertainment/tv/la-cast-tyler-perry-guided-tour-20161016-snap-story.html

- How to Collapse Reality (Quantum Decision Making). https://resistaverageacademy.com/quantum-decision-making/
- You Now Have a Shorter Attention Span Than a Goldfish. http://time.com/3858309/attention-spans-goldfish/

Chapter 9

- Marianne Williamson, *A Return to Love*. https://marianne.com/a-return-to-love/

Chapter 10

- Work Sucks: How the Movie "Office Space" Proves Radicalism Lives in the Mainstream. https://truthout.org/articles/work-sucks-an-old-film-favorite-proves-radicalism-lives-in-the-mainstream/
- Majority of Workers Are Unhappy Employees, Study Finds. https://www.theladders.com/career-advice/majority-unhappy-at-work
- What the Literature Says about the Earnings of Entrepreneurs. https://80000hours.org/2016/02/what-the-literature-says-about-the-earnings-of-entrepreneurs/
- James Altucher Podcast with Robert Kurson: https://jamesaltucher.com/2018/04/robert-kurson-the-leap-of-faith-everyone-needs-to-take/
- From the Kitchen to a Billion-Dollar Food Company, HustleCon. https://hustlecon.com/from-the-kitchen-to-a-billion-dollar-food-company/

Chapter 11

- Rich Roll, Finding Ultra. http://www.richroll.com/finding-ultra/
- Meet Rich Roll—One of 2009'S Men's Fitness Magazine's "25 Fittest Guys in the World," and Dedicated Vegan. http://www.vegsource.com/news/2009/11/meet-rich-roll—-one-of-2009s-mens-fitness-magazine-25-fittest-guys-in-the-world-and-dedicated-vegan.html

- Spark: The Revolutionary New Science of Exercise and the Brain, John Ratey. http://psycnet.apa.org/record/2008–02933–000
- Resist Average Academy, Ep 33: How to Forge an Unbeatable Mind, Body and Spirit with SEALFIT Founder Mark Divine. https://resistaverageacademy.com/ep-33-how-to-forge-an-unbeatable-mind-body-and-spirit-with-sealfit-founder-mark-divine/

Chapter 12

- Twitter CEO Jack Dorsey Tried the Meditation Craze That Requires No Sex, Drugs, or Talking for 10 days. Business Insider. www.businessinsider.com/twitter-ceo-jack-dorsey-does-vipassana-meditation-2018–1
- Why Silicon Valley Billionaires Are Obsessed with Burning Man, Vox. www.vox.com/2014/8/22/6050625/why-silicon-valley-billionaires-are-obsessed-with-burning-man
- Resist Average Academy, Ep. 59: How Floating Can Change Your Life with Shane Stott. https://resistaverageacademy.com/shanestott/
- The Tim Ferriss Show Transcripts: Meditation, Mindset, and Mastery. https://tim.blog/2018/06/20/the-tim-ferriss-show-transcripts-meditation-mindset-and-mastery/

Chapter 13

- School of Greatness Podcast by Lewis Howes, Ep. 697: Rachel Hollis. https://lewishowes.com/podcast/rachel-hollis-how-to-build-confidence-believe-in-yourself-and-become-your-best-self/
- Rise Together Podcast, with Rachel Hollis and Dave Hollis. "Why Hard Conversations Are Key to Building an Exceptional Relationship." https://www.risetogetherpodcast.com/episodes/
- Scott Stossel, "What Makes Us Happy, Revisited." *The Atlantic.* https://www.theatlantic.com/magazine/archive/2013/05/thanks-mom/309287/
- Brené Brown: The Power of Vulnerability TED Talk, 2010. https://www.ted.com/talks/brene_brown_on_vulnerability?language=en

Chapter 14

- Leap of Your Life Habit Worksheet: http://www.leapofyourlife.com

Chapter 15

- Benjamin P. Hardy, "How to Radically Change Your Goals and Success," *Inc.* https://www.inc.com/benjamin-p-hardy/how-to-10x-your-goals-and-success-.html

Chapter 16

- Leap of Your Life Declaration Form: http://www.leapofyourlife .com

Acknowledgments

First, I acknowledge you, the reader, who showed up and got to the end because it tells me a lot about who you are. I don't take that lightly, and I'm always humbled.

No book or creative work is done alone, and although plenty of mornings started out at 3:30 a.m. in the darkness, it took a team. To my fiancée Taylor, thank you for being a support system during the tough stretches. I love you so much and there's no way this exists without you.

This work started out as a *feeling* I couldn't not express. Then, it took shape because of all the people I had conversations with or consulted directly with. This includes: Lisa Nichols, Lisa Terner, Kelly Exeter, Debbie Reber, Jeff Goins, Mike Zeller, Marion Roach, Jim Steg, Seth Mattison, Shannon Graham, Jay Nixon, Brandon Duncan, and several others.

Thank you to both Megan Nichols and John Hill for extensive early research. Thank you to all of my mentors, including Dr. John Demartini. A deep hearted thank you to all my incredible clients from the past, the present and the future; your trust in my work and ability to guide you means the world, and I'm honored to walk this path with you.

I want to thank the entire publishing team at Wiley who put up with my unabashed enthusiasm (sometimes, to my own detriment) and helped keep me sane. Thank you to Richard Narramore for taking a chance, and to Vicki Adang for helping me improve the messaging and delivery.

To all the podcast guests who have been part of the Resist Average Academy: your message is part of this, too. Your willingness to share your challenges and bold steps into the unknown made all the difference. You have all inspired me with your willingness and courage. Thank you for treating our conversations as authentically as you did.

Lastly, I'm often asked about who my mentors are. And while I can rattle off a list, they don't hold a candle to my parents: thank you from the bottom of my heart. I quite often feel as if I won the parent lottery. None of this happens without you.

Index

Note: Page references in *italics* refer to figures.